VEGETABLES THE FRENCH WAY

VEGETABLES

THE FRENCH WAY

JACK SANTA MARIA

Illustrated by Oliver Caldecott

HEALING ARTS PRESS

Rochester, Vermont

Healing Arts Press
One Park Street
Rochester, Vermont 05767

Copyright © 1989 Jack Santa Maria

LIBRARY OF CONGRESS CATALOGING IN PUBLICATION DATA
Santa Maria, Jack.
  Vegetables the French way / Jack Santa Maria ; illustrated by Oliver Caldecott. — 1st U.S. ed.
    p.   cm.
  ISBN 0-89281-331-8 :
  1. Cookery (Vegetables)   2. Cookery, French.   I. Caldecott, Oliver.   II. Title.
TX801.S26   1989
641.6'5 — dc20   89–15546
                                                            CIP

Printed and bound in the United States

10 9 8 7 6 5 4 3 2 1

Healing Arts Press is a division of Inner Traditions International, Ltd.

Distributed to the book trade in Canada by Book Center, Inc., Montreal, Quebec
Distributed to the health food trade in Canada by Alive Books, Toronto and Vancouver

Contents

Acknowledgments

I would like to thank many French friends for their hospitality during my stays in France, especially Sally Guéret; also the Vegetarian Society for their help. I am grateful to those who have freely given their constructive criticism and suggestions during the compilation of the book and to my editor, Oliver Caldecott, for his continuing moral support.

Introduction

France is a large, fertile country with a variety of climates and soils, from the cool temperate north with its lush woods and pastures to the hot Mediterranean south with its olive groves and mountain slopes covered with aromatic herbs. These factors have had a profound effect on a cuisine which is distinctly regional in flavor and at the same time internationally recognizable as French.

In the countryside the approach to vegetables is simple and direct and they are generally an accompaniment to meat, game or fish. However, many of the classic vegetable soups and casseroles may form the basis of a meal in their own right. French cooks like to buy their vegetables as fresh as possible, on the day they are to be used. Always choose the best quality to get the best results. Vegetables should be bright and firm with no hint of limpness or dullness of color. It is their fresh aroma which gives their wholesome taste so that they need to be chosen carefully. Like wine, the taste and bouquet are related to the quality.

Though French cuisine is one of the most sophisticated in the world, like all great cuisines its origins spring from the robust cooking of the farm and country home. This classic repertoire, known as *cuisine ancienne traditionelle*, has been the inspirational base for the great creative chefs. The French are proud of this tradition, for it has allowed and encouraged a vigorous cuisine which can evolve and grow.

For many centuries cooking techniques were influenced by the wood- or coal-burning stove. Then, as the modern stove became more refined, people moved away from the farms and villages to live in larger towns and cities. With this movement came a demand for new and faster cooking techniques. Since the Second World War, France has steadily grown more affluent and this has become evident in an important new development which has come about in the last fifteen years. Like important movements in painting, this development sought and found a fresh approach to the preparation and presentation of food, now known as *Nouvelle Cuisine*.

Here, the accent is not only on new ingredients and combinations, but also on form and color. A principle dedication is to a "lyrical lightness" and a regard for the uniqueness of each ingredient. The final serving has drawn much inspiration from Japan with arresting elements of pattern and stillness, bringing a new sense of delight to the table. Nouvelle Cuisine also demonstrates a new attitude to vegetables. Their form, color and texture are given an equal place with the other main ingredients.

Building on the discoveries of Nouvelle Cuisine, Michel Guérard's *Cuisine Minceur* (1977) answered the modern need to reduce the calorie content of French food. The reduction of cream and butter is combined with smaller portions, shorter cooking times for vegetables and a greater use of raw food (*crudités*). Since then, he and other chefs have created another facet of the new cuisine which Guérard calls *Cuisine Gourmande*. This seeks to blend the richness of the classic tradition with contemporary innovations. Whatever opinions may be, any renaissance in the world of cooking brings with it the beneficial elements of controversy, discussion and experiment. It is therefore an exciting time in which to investigate the French way with vegetables.

Naturally, the advent of the new techniques has generated criticism. Among the many positive benefits, however, is that French people are looking with new eyes at the traditional base of their contemporary cooking. This book presents a view of this tradition, as it concerns vegetables, along with some of the new developments. Be prepared to use whatever is at hand, to vary ingredients and to be experimental, for this is how the cooks of France came to create and continue to create their unique style.

Artichokes

The artichoke was brought to France from Sicily by Catherine de Medici and has been cultivated there since the sixteenth century. The main areas of cultivation today are the west of Brittany, Anjou, Provence, the valley of the Garonne, Paris and Roussillon in the south. Especially prized are the large green artichoke of Laon, the *camus* of Brittany and the violet and green of Provence. Artichokes are considered to be at their most delicious when eaten raw, while young and tender *à la croque-au-sel*, with nothing but a pinch of salt.

Artichokes with French Dressing
(*Artichauts à la Vinaigrette*)   Serves 4

4 large *or* 8 small artichokes
6 tablespoons olive oil
2 tablespoons wine vinegar
Salt

Freshly ground black pepper
½ teaspoon Dijon mustard
1 teaspoon chopped fresh herbs

Cut off any stem of the artichokes and pull off any hard outer leaves. Cut across the top and scoop out the hairy "choke." Cut off any remaining sharp tips to any leaves. Put in steamer and cook until the artichokes are just tender (30–45 minutes).

Meanwhile, prepare the dressing. Whisk together the rest of the ingredients. The proportions may be varied to suit individual taste but the dressing should not be too sharp. Crushed or finely chopped garlic could be substituted for the herbs. Cool the cooked artichokes under cold water and place on a serving dish. Put a little of the dressing in the center of each artichoke. Serve chilled or at room temperature.

Stuffed Artichokes
(Artichauts Farcis)

4 large artichokes
Juice of 1 lemon
2 tablespoons melted butter
2 tablespoons sliced button
  mushrooms
2 garlic cloves, finely chopped *or*
  crushed

3 tablespoons fresh whole wheat
  breadcrumbs
3 tablespoons chopped parsley
2 tablespoons olive oil
Salt
Freshly ground black pepper

Cut off any stem of the artichokes and pull off the hard outer leaves.
Cut across the top and scoop out the hairy "choke." This is the cavity
that will be stuffed. Cut off any remaining sharp tips to any leaves. Put
the prepared artichokes in a bowl of cold water and lemon juice.

Heat the butter in a heavy pan and gently sauté the mushrooms for
two minutes. Add the rest of the ingredients and sauté together for three
or more minutes. Remove the artichokes from the lemon water and
drain. Put a portion of the stuffing in each artichoke. Arrange them in a
pan which can just hold them in one layer. Pour in water to just cover
the bottom of the artichokes. Cover and simmer or steam until the
artichokes are just tender (30–45 minutes). Serve hot or cold.

These stuffed artichokes may also be baked in a medium oven until
tender. Sprinkle with a little more oil before baking and bake in an
ovenproof dish for about one hour.

Artichokes in Cream Sauce
(Artichauts à la Crème)

4 large artichokes
Lemon juice
3 tablespoons melted butter
2 tablespoons whole wheat flour
½ cup plain yogurt

½ cup thick cream
Salt
Freshly ground black *or* white
  pepper
1 tablespoon chopped parsley

Prepare the artichokes as in the previous recipe and cut each one in quarters. Sprinkle with a little lemon juice. Heat 2 tablespoons of butter in a heavy pan and add the artichokes. Turn them gently in the butter then cover with water and cook until the artichoke pieces are tender. Remove from heat and keep warm. Heat the rest of the butter in another pan and stir in the flour. When it just begins to turn color, stir in the yogurt, then the cream. Add salt and pepper to taste. Add any juice in the artichoke pan and cook the sauce together until it thickens. Put in the artichokes to allow them to warm through. Pour onto a serving dish and serve garnished with the parsley.

Artichokes with Peas and Lettuce
(Artichauts Clamart)   Serves 6

In the days of the monarchy the *petits pois* supplied to the homes of noble Parisians came from the market gardens at Clamart. If the peas and lettuce are replaced by the same quantity of young carrots, you have the dish *Artichauts Crécy* which takes its name from the town of Crécy in Seine-et-Marne, where high quality carrots are grown.

12 small young artichokes	Salt
1/3 cup butter	Freshly ground black *or* white
1 1/4 cups peas	pepper
2 lettuce hearts, shredded	1 teaspoon soft brown sugar

Prepare the artichokes as in the previous recipes. Heat the butter in a heavy pan and turn artichokes in the melted butter. Add the peas and lettuce. Season with salt and pepper to taste and add the sugar. Sprinkle with 3–4 tablespoons of water. Cover and simmer until the artichokes are tender (15–30 minutes). Serve basted with melted butter, adding more at the end if needed.

Artichoke Stew
(*Ragoût d'Artichauts*)

Serves 6

6 large *or* 12 small young
   artichokes
Lemon juice
2 tablespoons melted butter
2 tablespoons olive oil
1 onion, chopped
3 large tomatoes, chopped

1 teaspoon chopped marjoram
1 teaspoon chopped basil
2 teaspoons chopped parsley
Salt
Freshly ground black pepper
2¼ cups vegetable stock

Prepare the artichokes as in the previous recipes. Cut each artichoke in quarters and sprinkle with lemon juice. Heat the butter and oil in a heavy pan and add the onions. Simmer until the onions begin to turn golden. Add the artichokes, tomatoes, marjoram and basil and turn in the oil. Sprinkle with the parsley and season with salt and pepper to taste. Stir in the stock and stew the dish gently until the artichokes are tender. Turn out onto a serving dish or serve straight from the pot.

Artichoke Gratin
(*Gratin d'Artichauts*)

Serves 4

4 large artichokes
Lemon juice
7 tablespoons olive oil
1 onion, chopped
3 cloves garlic, finely chopped
1 tablespoon chopped parsley
1 teaspoon chopped marjoram

1 teaspoon chopped basil
1 cup whole wheat breadcrumbs
Salt
Freshly ground black pepper
2-3 tablespoons grated parmesan
   cheese

Prepare the artichokes as in the previous recipes. Put in a bowl and sprinkle with lemon juice. Preheat the oven to 400°F. Smear an oven-proof dish with 1 tablespoon of oil. Mix together the onion, garlic, herbs and breadcrumbs with salt and pepper to taste. Stir in 4 tablespoons of oil. Put half of the breadcrumb mixture in the greased dish. Drain the artichokes and cut each one into quarters. Put the artichoke pieces on the breadcrumb layer. Cover with the rest of the breadcrumb mixture. Sprinkle with the cheese. Dribble the rest of the oil over the surface and bake for 15 minutes. Turn down the heat to 375°F and continue baking until the top is crisp and golden (about 1 hour).

Asparagus

A member of the lily family, asparagus grows wild over large parts of France, especially on poor or sandy soils. It became popular during the reign of the Sun King, Louis XIV, and has remained so in spite of its high price.

Asparagus Salad
(*Salade d'Asperges*)

Serves 4

Asparagus is a delicious vegetable to eat on its own with just a little melted butter. Here, this simplicity is incorporated into a plain salad.

2 pounds asparagus
Salt
1 small iceberg lettuce, shredded
4 scallions, thinly sliced
2 stalks celery

2 tablespoons chopped cucumber
2 tablespoons chopped parsley *or* watercress
2 teaspoons chopped herbs
½ cup (1 stick) butter

Clean the asparagus stalks and trim to about 8–9 inches in length. Put in a steamer and sprinkle with a little salt. You may find it easier to handle the cooked asparagus if the stalks are tied in small bundles with thick thread or string. Steam until the stalks are tender (8–12 minutes).

Meanwhile, prepare the rest of the salad. Mix together the salad ingredients and put in the center of a serving dish. Melt the butter in a heavy saucepan and pour over the asparagus. Arrange the stalks around the edge of the dish. Do not make up a dressing but supply olive oil, wine vinegar, salt and fresh pepper so that the dressing can be made up to taste.

Baked Asparagus
(Asperges au Four)

Serves 4

1 pound asparagus
Salt
2 tablespoons olive oil
2 tablespoons butter
1 onion, chopped
3 large tomatoes, sliced
2 zucchini, trimmed and sliced
2 cloves garlic, finely chopped

1 teaspoon chopped oregano
1 teaspoon chopped parsley
Freshly ground black pepper
2 tablespoons whole wheat
  breadcrumbs
2 tablespoons grated parmesan
  cheese

Prepare and steam the asparagus until it is tender as in the recipe for Asparagus Salad. Meanwhile heat the oil and butter in a heavy pan and sauté the onion until it begins to turn golden. Add the tomatoes, zucchini, garlic, herbs, and salt and pepper to taste. Stir together well. Preheat the oven to 400°F.

When the zucchini are tender, arrange the asparagus and tomato mixture in layers in an ovenproof dish. Mix together the breadcrumbs and cheese and sprinkle on the top of the dish. Bake in the oven until the top is golden (15–20 minutes).

Asparagus Touraine-Style
(Asperges à la Tourangelle)

Serves 6

At the heart of the château country, the province of Touraine is known as the garden of France. The asparagus of the region is particularly good and is featured here in the local style.

2 pounds asparagus
3 tablespoons melted butter
1 tablespoon olive oil
1 onion, sliced
2 cups vegetable stock
1 tablespoon whole wheat flour

Salt
Freshly ground white or black
  pepper
1 tablespoon chopped parsley
1 iceberg lettuce heart, shredded

Trim the asparagus and cut into short lengths. Heat the butter and oil in a heavy pan and gently sauté the onion until transparent. Add the asparagus and turn in the oil. Add a little stock to the flour in a cup and stir together until there are no lumps. Pour into the pan with the rest of the stock. Add salt and pepper to taste and the chopped parsley. Cover and simmer together for 10 minutes. Remove the lid and sprinkle the lettuce over. Cover and continue cooking until the asparagus is tender. Serve hot.

Asparagus Soup
(*Crème d'Asperges*)   Serves 6

1 pound asparagus
Salt
1 tablespoon olive oil
1 tablespoon melted butter
1 onion, chopped
2 tablespoons whole wheat *or*
  potato flour

2¼ cups vegetable stock
2¼ cups milk
2 teaspoons chopped herbs
Freshly ground black pepper
½ cup heavy cream *or* yogurt

Clean and trim the asparagus and cook in slightly salted water just enough to cover the stalks. Simmer and retain the liquid.

Meanwhile, heat the oil and butter in a heavy pan and gently sauté the onion until transparent. Add the flour and stir together well. Slowly add the stock, then the milk. Stir in the herbs and pepper to taste and allow to simmer.

Remove the cooked asparagus from the water and trim off the tips. Cut the rest of the stalks into short pieces and add to the soup, keeping the tips to one side. Add some of the asparagus water if the soup is too thick. Blend the soup in a blender, put back in the pan to reheat and add the cream. Do not allow the soup to boil. Serve garnished with the asparagus tips.

Asparagus in Cream Sauce
(*Asperges à la Crème*) Serves 4

This dish needs to be prepared as near as possible to serving since reheating causes curdling.

1 pound asparagus
Salt
¼ cup (½ stick) butter
2 egg yolks
¼ cup milk

1 teaspoon chopped parsley
1 teaspoon chopped tarragon
Freshly ground white *or* black
    pepper
1 cup heavy cream

Prepare and steam the asparagus until tender as in the recipe for Asparagus Salad. Melt the butter in a heavy pan and turn the cooked asparagus in the butter. Keep warm on one side.

Beat the egg yolks together with a fork in a heavy saucepan and add the milk, herbs, and salt and pepper to taste. Gently heat until the mixture begins to bubble. Drain off any excess butter from the asparagus and add to the mixture. Add the cream and allow the mixture to become hot. Put the asparagus on a serving dish and pour the sauce over. Serve immediately.

Beets

Beets were first brought to France by the Romans, who used the leaves as a vegetable. The root is now used both as a cooked vegetable and in salads. Clean the root and boil in fresh water until tender. Peel off the skin.

Beet Salad
(Salade de Betteraves)   Serves 4

½ pound beets, cooked
1 tablespoon wine vinegar
Salt
Freshly ground black pepper

½ teaspoon Dijon mustard
3 tablespoons olive oil
1–2 tablespoons chopped walnuts

Slice the beets or dice and put in a salad bowl. Make the vinaigrette by whisking together the vinegar, a pinch of salt and pepper and the mustard. Gradually whisk in the oil until the sauce is well blended. Mix with the beets. Sprinkle with the walnuts just before serving.

If a strong taste is desired, allow the beets to stand in the vinaigrette for up to an hour without the nuts.

Beet and Mint Salad
(Salade de Betteraves à la Menthe)   Serves 4

This salad is adapted from the Roman dish which used the red leaves of beets with various green herbs.

½ pound beets, cooked and
  diced
1 large red eating apple, cored
  and chopped
4 scallions, sliced
Lemon juice
½ cup natural yogurt

1 tablespoon heavy cream
1–2 tablespoons chopped fresh
  mint
Salt
Freshly ground black pepper
A few sprigs of watercress

Mix the beets, apple and scallions together in a bowl. Sprinkle a little lemon juice over to just coat the vegetables. In a separate bowl mix together the yogurt, cream, and salt and pepper to taste. Arrange the beet mixture on a salad dish. Make a space in the center and pour in the yogurt and mint mixture. Garnish with sprigs of watercress. Crème fraîche may be used instead of the yogurt.

Creamed Beets
(Betteraves à la Crème)   Serves 4

¾ pound beets, cooked
2 tablespoons melted butter
½ cup natural yogurt
½ cup heavy cream

2 teaspoons chopped tarragon
Salt
Freshly ground white *or* black
  pepper

Warm the cooked beets in the butter and keep warm to one side. In a heavy pan gently heat the yogurt and cream. Add the tarragon and salt and pepper to taste. Gently stir in the beets and butter. Heat through but do not allow the cream sauce to boil.

Beets with Onions
(*Betteraves aux Oignons*)

Serves 4

1 onion, finely chopped
2 tablespoons butter
1 tablespoon olive oil
½ pound beets, cooked and
    chopped

½ cup natural yogurt
Salt
Freshly ground black pepper
2 teaspoons chopped parsley
2 teaspoons chopped chives

Put the onion in a heavy pan with the butter and oil and gently sauté until the onion is transparent. Stir in the beets and fold in the oil. Add the yogurt and salt and pepper to taste. Warm through and serve garnished with the parsley and chives.

Broccoli

Broccoli and Potatoes
(Brocolis aux Pommes de Terre)　　　　　Serves 4

2 tablespoons olive oil
1 tablespoon melted butter
1 small onion, sliced
1 pound potatoes, parcooked and
　cut in pieces
1 pound broccoli, trimmed and
　cut in pieces

1 clove garlic, finely chopped
Salt
Freshly ground black pepper
1 cup water

Heat the oil and butter in a heavy pan and gently sauté the onion until it just begins to turn golden. Add the potatoes and allow to cook for 5 minutes. Add the broccoli, garlic, salt and pepper to taste and water. Cover and cook together until the broccoli is tender. Test by prodding the stem with a fork. Serve hot.

Broccoli with Butter Sauce
(Brocolis au Beurre)　　　　　Serves 4

1½ pounds broccoli, trimmed
　and cut in pieces
Salt

4 tablespoons melted butter
Freshly ground black pepper
2 teaspoons chopped parsley

Wash the broccoli and put in a steamer. Sprinkle with a little salt and steam until the broccoli is tender. Heat the butter in a heavy pan and season with pepper and chopped parsley. When the butter is well seasoned put in the broccoli and turn well in the butter until it is well covered. Serve immediately.

Broccoli and Vegetable Stew
(*Ragoût de Brocolis aux Légumes*)

Serves 4

2 tablespoons melted butter
2 tablespoons olive oil
1 onion, chopped
½ pound potatoes, chopped
1 pound broccoli, trimmed and sliced
½ pound zucchini, sliced

1 cup vegetable stock
1 cup wine
Salt
Freshly ground black pepper
2 teaspoons chopped parsley
1 teaspoon chopped tarragon
2 teaspoons chopped chives

Heat the butter and oil in a heavy pan and sauté the onion until transparent. Add the potatoes and turn in the oil for 3 minutes. Add the broccoli, zucchini, stock, wine and salt and pepper to taste and cook together for 5 minutes. Add the parsley and tarragon. Cover and simmer until the potatoes are tender. Serve hot garnished with chopped chives.

Brussels Sprouts

Brussels Sprouts Purée
(*Purée de Choux de Bruxelles*)   Serves 6

Brussels sprouts may be cooked and puréed on their own. The traditional French way is to add puréed potato to the Brussels sprouts, which
gives the mixture more body.

2 pounds Brussels sprouts	1 pound potatoes
Salt	Freshly ground black pepper
½ cup (1 stick) butter	Pinch freshly grated nutmeg

Trim the sprouts and cook in slightly salted boiling water until just
tender. Heat half of the butter in a heavy pan and turn the sprouts in
the melted butter. Purée the sprouts in a blender or food processor and
keep warm.

Meanwhile, cook the potatoes in a little water until they are tender.
Peel. Purée in a blender and add the rest of the butter to the potatoes.
Mix the puréed sprouts and potatoes together in a bowl, adding salt and
pepper to taste. Serve sprinkled with a little grated nutmeg.

Other vegetables may be puréed in this simple way, such as carrots,
rutabagas or parsnips.

Brussels Sprouts Gratin
(*Gratin de Choux de Bruxelles*)   Serves 4

1 pound Brussels sprouts
Salt
2 tablespoons melted butter
4 eggs
½ cup natural yogurt *or* crème
  fraîche

Freshly ground black pepper
4 tablespoons whole wheat
  breadcrumbs
2 tablespoons olive oil

Preheat the oven to 400°F. Trim the sprouts and boil in slightly salted water for 5 minutes. Drain and chop in a mixing bowl. Grease the bottom and sides of a gratin dish with butter.

While the sprouts are cooking, boil the eggs in water for 10 minutes. Remove the shells and chop. Add to the chopped sprouts and stir in the yogurt and salt and pepper to taste. Put in the buttered gratin dish and cover with the breadcrumbs. Sprinkle the olive oil over and bake in the oven until the top is crisp and golden (20–30 minutes).

Cabbage

In Alsace on Maundy Thursday (Jeudi Saint) nothing but green vegetables may be eaten. Among these, the cabbage takes pride of place.

Cabbage Lorraine-Style
(*Chou à la Lorraine*)   Serves 4

This is typical of the robust mountain cooking to be found in this part of eastern France.

1½ pounds cabbage
Salt
4 tablespoons olive oil
1 onion, sliced
1¼ cups chopped tomatoes
1 tablespoon whole wheat flour
1 cup vegetable stock

½ cup wine
½ cup crème fraîche *or* natural
   yogurt
Freshly ground black pepper
1 teaspoon chopped parsley
1 teaspoon chopped marjoram

Trim the cabbage and cut into quarters. Wash in cold water and cook in slightly salted water for 5 minutes. Drain. Heat the oil in a heavy pan and gently sauté the onion until transparent. Add the tomatoes and turn in the oil for 3 minutes. Add a little stock to the flour in a cup and stir together. Pour into the pan with the rest of the stock. Put in the drained cabbage and pour the wine over. Stir in the crème fraîche, salt and pepper to taste and herbs. Cover and cook together until the cabbage is just tender.

Cabbage Loaf
(*Pain au Chou*)

Serves 6

2 pounds cabbage
Salt
2 heaping tablespoons whole
   wheat flour
Freshly ground black pepper

1 tablespoon olive oil
3 eggs
½ cup milk
Freshly grated nutmeg
Butter

For the white sauce (*sauce velouté*):
2½ tablespoons butter
¼ cup whole wheat flour
2 cups milk
½ cup cream

Salt
Freshly ground white pepper
Lemon juice

Trim the cabbage and cut into quarters. Wash in cold water. Boil in slightly salted water until the cabbage is tender. Drain and chop well. In a mixing bowl, sift together the flour, a pinch of salt and a little pepper. Stir in the olive oil. Beat the eggs and stir into the flour. Slowly stir in the milk. Cover with a damp cloth and let stand for 30 minutes. 10 minutes before the end of this time, preheat the oven to 400°F.

Stir the chopped cabbage into the batter and sprinkle a little grated nutmeg over. Put the mixture into a well-buttered ovenproof dish and bake in the oven until the loaf is well set (30–40 minutes). Keep warm while you prepare the sauce.

Melt the butter in a heavy pan over low heat. Stir in the flour and stir together for 2 minutes. In sauce making, this is known as the white *roux*. Remove the roux from the heat. As soon as the roux has stopped bubbling whisk in the milk, which should be very hot but not boiling. Whisk well until the sauce is well blended. You now have the sauce velouté. This is enriched to go with the cabbage loaf by beating in the cream by the spoonful. Keep the sauce simmering and add salt, pepper and lemon juice to taste. Pour over slices of the cabbage loaf.

Red Cabbage Salad
(*Salade de Chou Rouge*)

Serves 4

2½ cups red cabbage, shredded
1 tablespoon sliced onion
2 tablespoons sliced radishes
2 tablespoons chopped walnuts
1 tablespoon wine vinegar

Salt
Freshly ground black pepper
½ teaspoon Dijon mustard
3 tablespoons olive oil

Put washed and shredded cabbage into a salad bowl. Add the onions, radishes and walnuts. In a separate bowl whisk together the vinegar with a pinch of salt and pepper and the mustard. Gradually whisk in the oil. Pour the vinaigrette over the red cabbage salad. Allow to stand for 1 hour before serving.

Cabbage Purée
(*Purée de Chou*)

Serves 4

2 pounds cabbage
1 onion, sliced
Pinch chopped thyme
Pinch chopped marjoram
Pinch chopped basil
2 tablespoons melted butter

2 tablespoons heavy cream
Salt
Freshly ground black pepper
Pinch freshly grated nutmeg
Sliced apples, to garnish

Trim the cabbage and slice. Boil in a little water with the onion and herbs. When the cabbage is tender, purée in a blender or food processor. Put into a serving bowl and stir in the butter, cream, salt and pepper to taste. Sprinkle with a little grated nutmeg. Serve with sliced apples.

Stuffed Cabbage Leaves
(*Feuilles de Chou Farcies*)

Serves 4

1 large Savoy cabbage
Salt
1 pound potatoes
1 onion, finely chopped
2 tablespoons melted butter
1 tablespoon olive oil

2 cloves garlic, finely chopped
4 tablespoons whole wheat
    breadcrumbs
2 hard-boiled eggs, chopped
1 tablespoon chopped herbs
Freshly ground black pepper

Wash and trim the cabbage, discarding any damaged outer leaves. Break off up to 16 leaves and carefully place in a pan. Just cover with a little slightly salted water and boil gently until the leaves are tender. Lift them carefully from the pan and allow to drain. Meanwhile boil the potatoes in slightly salted water until tender. Peel and mash.

In another pan gently sauté the onion in the butter and oil until transparent. Add the garlic and breadcrumbs and cook together for 3 minutes. Stir in the eggs, herbs and salt and pepper to taste, then the mashed potato. Mix together well.

Lay out each cabbage leaf, stem downward and place a portion of the stuffing mixture in the center. Fold up like an envelope. Place the cabbage envelopes in a steamer and steam for 5 minutes to warm through. Serve hot or cold.

Braised Red Cabbage
(*Chou Rouge Braisé*)

Serves 4

A good Burgundy wine is an essential ingredient in this recipe from the Ardennes in northern France.

1 medium-sized red cabbage
2 tablespoons melted butter
1 tablespoon olive oil
1 onion, sliced
1 tablespoon brown sugar

1 tablespoon wine vinegar
½ cup dry red wine
Salt
Freshly ground black pepper

Preheat the oven to 350°F. Trim the cabbage and shred fine. Heat the butter and oil in a heavy pan and stir in the onion. Sauté over low heat until transparent. Add the sugar and stir together until the sugar caramelizes. Add the cabbage and vinegar and stir together. Add the wine and salt and pepper to taste. Cover the pan and bake in the oven until the cabbage is tender (about 45 minutes). Remove the lid 10 minutes before the end of the cooking to allow the excess moisture to evaporate.

Braised Cabbage
(*Chou Braisé*)   Serves 4

1½ pounds cabbage
Salt
2 tablespoons melted butter
2 tablespoons olive oil

1 onion, sliced
1½ cups vegetable stock
½ cup wine
Freshly ground black pepper

Trim the cabbage and cut in quarters. Wash well in cold water and boil in slightly salted water for 5 minutes. Drain. Heat the butter and oil in a heavy pan and gently sauté the onion until transparent. Add the cabbage and turn in the oil. Add the stock, wine and salt and pepper to taste. Cook together for a few more minutes until the cabbage is tender. Do not allow the cabbage to soften.

Red Cabbage with Chestnuts
(*Chou Rouge aux Marrons*)   Serves 4

This dish is popular in the region of Limousin where there are still forests of chestnut trees.

½ pound fresh chestnuts
1 pound red cabbage
¼ cup (½ stick) butter
2 tablespoons red wine vinegar
1 cup vegetable stock

Salt
Freshly ground black pepper
1 large cooking apple, peeled,
   cored and chopped
1 tablespoon soft brown sugar

Make a slit in each of the chestnuts and boil in water until tender. Skin the chestnuts, allow to cool and slice. Trim the cabbage, quarter and slice. Heat the butter in a heavy pan and sauté the cabbage for 3 minutes. Add the chestnuts, vinegar, stock, salt and pepper to taste, apple and sugar. Stir together and cover. Simmer for 15 minutes. Serve hot.

Carrots

Carrot Soufflé
(Soufflé aux Carottes)   Serves 4

Butter
3 tablespoons grated parmesan
   cheese
1 pound carrots, peeled and
   chopped

Salt
2 tablespoons flour
1⅛ cups milk
3 eggs and 1 egg white
Freshly ground white pepper

Prepare the soufflé dish by smearing the inside with butter and coating with grated parmesan cheese. Tie a band of buttered waxed or parchment paper around the outside of the dish so that it is about 2 inches higher than the edge.

Cook the carrots in boiling, slightly salted water until tender. Drain. Purée in a food processor or put through a food mill. Return the purée to the pan and allow the excess moisture to evaporate over low heat. Remove from the heat. Preheat the oven to 400°F.

Melt 2 tablespoons of butter in another saucepan and add the flour. Stir together for 2 minutes over low heat, then gradually stir in the milk. Bring to a boil, stirring continuously for 7 minutes. Add the carrot purée and allow to cool. Separate the egg yolks from the whites and add the yolks to the carrot mixture. Stir in salt and pepper to taste. Whisk the 4 egg whites until stiff. Fold 1 tablespoon of egg white into the carrot mixture, then carefully fold in the remaining whites in three amounts. Pour the whole mixture into the prepared soufflé dish. Bake until the soufflé rises (20–25 minutes). Serve immediately.

Carrot Soup
(Potage aux Carottes)   Serves 6

2 tablespoons olive oil
1 onion, finely chopped
1 pound carrots, chopped
2 cups chopped potatoes
7¼ cups water *or* thin vegetable
  stock

Salt
Freshly ground black pepper
1 tablespoon chopped parsley

Heat the oil in a heavy soup pot and gently sauté the onion until transparent. Add the carrots and potatoes and turn in the oil for 3 minutes. Pour in the water or stock and season with salt and pepper to taste. Cover and cook until the vegetables are tender. Purée in a blender or food processor. Serve hot, garnished with chopped parsley.

This soup is excellent with chunks of bread or croûtons.

Carrot Purée
(Purée de Carottes)   Serves 6

3 pounds carrots
Salt
3 tablespoons melted butter
1 small onion, finely chopped

Freshly ground black pepper
1 teaspoon chopped tarragon
3 tablespoons heavy cream

Trim the carrots and peel. Chop and boil in slightly salted water until the carrots are tender. Purée in a blender or food processor. Put back in the pan and add salt and pepper to taste, tarragon, melted butter and cream. Heat the purée gently but do not allow it to bubble.

Carrots with Scallions
(*Carottes aux Ciboules*)

Serves 4

1 pound carrots
Salt
3 tablespoons melted butter
1 bunch scallions, chopped

1⅓ cups frozen peas
1 cup vegetable stock
Freshly ground black pepper
A few sage leaves

Peel and trim the carrots and slice. Boil in slightly salted water until almost tender. Drain. Heat the butter in a heavy pan and gently sauté the scallions for 2 minutes. Add the carrots and peas along with the stock, salt and pepper to taste and sage leaves. Cover and cook together until the carrots are tender.

Glazed Carrots
(*Carottes Glacées*)

Serves 2

8 baby carrots
2¼ cups stock *or* water
2½ tablespoons butter
1-2 teaspoons confectioner's
  sugar

Pinch salt
Freshly ground black pepper

Peel the carrots as necessary and trim off most of the green leaves. Put the carrots in a saucepan which just allows them to lie flat. Add the stock, butter, sugar and salt and pepper to taste. Allow to simmer until most of the liquid has evaporated (20 minutes), leaving the carrots glazed with a thick syrup.

Carrots Provence-Style
(*Carottes à la Provençale*)

3 tablespoons melted butter
3 tablespoons olive oil
1 onion, chopped
1 pound carrots, sliced
½ pound tomatoes, chopped
½ pound zucchini, sliced
2-4 cloves garlic, finely chopped

6-10 olives, pitted and sliced
2 teaspoons chopped parsley
2 teaspoons chopped basil
½ cup water *or* vegetable stock
½ cup wine
Salt
Freshly ground black pepper

Heat the butter and oil in a heavy pan and gently sauté the onion until transparent. Add the carrots, tomatoes, zucchini, garlic and olives and turn in the oil for 2 minutes. Add the herbs, stock, wine and salt and pepper to taste. Cover and simmer until the carrots are tender.

Cauliflower

Cauliflower has been known in Italy since the sixteenth century from where it was brought to France. It should always be bought when the leaves are green since this is a freshness indicator.

Cauliflower Fritters
(*Beignets de Chou-fleur*)
Serves 4

1 pound cauliflower
1 egg, beaten
1½ tablespoons whole wheat
  flour
Pinch baking powder
Pinch salt
Pinch freshly ground black
  pepper

4 tablespoons olive oil
1 tablespoon lemon juice
1 tablespoon chopped fresh herbs
Oil for deep frying
1 lemon, cut into wedges

Trim the cauliflower and cut into small florets. Wash well in cold water and drain well. Make up the fritter batter by beating together the egg, flour, baking powder, salt and pepper with a little water to make a thin, creamy consistency. Allow to stand for 30 minutes.

Meanwhile, make up a marinade for the cauliflower. Mix together the olive oil, lemon juice and herbs. Turn the cauliflower sprigs in this marinade and allow to stand until the batter is ready. Heat the oil in a deep pan until it is quite hot. Put the sprigs into the batter and make sure they are well coated. Remove from batter and fry in the hot oil until golden. Remove with a slotted spoon and allow to drain on paper towels. Serve with lemon wedges.

Cauliflower Salad
(*Salade de Chou-fleur*)

Serves 4

1 pound cauliflower
2 tablespoons blanched and
   sliced almonds

2 teaspoons chopped tarragon

For the mayonnaise:
2 egg yolks
2 tablespoons white wine vinegar
1 teaspoon dry *or* Dijon mustard
Salt

Freshly ground white pepper
1¼ cups sunflower oil

Trim the cauliflower and break into small florets. Wash well in cold water and drain. Put in a bowl and stir in the almonds.

Meanwhile, make sure that all the mayonnaise ingredients are at room temperature so that they will blend properly. Beat the egg yolks in a bowl with half of the vinegar. Beat in the mustard, salt and pepper to taste until the mixture thickens. Whisk in the oil drop by drop. After 2 tablespoons of oil have been added the mixture should be quite thick. Keep adding the rest of the oil gradually. Check the seasoning, adding the rest of the vinegar if this taste is desired. Serve at room temperature. 1 tablespoon of lemon juice may be substituted for the wine vinegar. Olive oil or other vegetable oil may be substituted for the sunflower oil.

Stir the mayonnaise into the cauliflower and sprinkle the tarragon over.

Cauliflower with Egg and Breadcrumbs
(*Chou-fleur à la Polonaise*)

Serves 4

1 good-sized cauliflower
¼ cup (½ stick) butter
3 tablespoons whole wheat
   breadcrumbs
Salt

Freshly ground black pepper
1 hard-boiled egg, finely
   chopped
1 tablespoon chopped parsley

Trim the cauliflower and cut into florets. Wash well and cook in boiling water until just tender. Drain and put in a greased ovenproof dish. Melt the butter in a heavy pan and sauté the breadcrumbs until they begin to turn golden. Mix in salt and pepper to taste and sprinkle over the cauliflower. Put under the broiler for 5 minutes to heat through. Garnish with the egg and parsley. Serve hot.

Cauliflower with Cheese Sauce
(*Chou-fleur au Gratin*)   Serves 4

1 good-sized cauliflower
Salt
3 tablespoons butter
1 onion, sliced
2 tablespoons whole wheat flour
1½ cups grated gruyère *or* cheddar cheese

Freshly ground black pepper
½ teaspoon chopped oregano
½ teaspoon chopped marjoram
½ teaspoon dry *or* Dijon mustard
Pinch grated nutmeg

Trim the cauliflower and cut into florets. Wash well in cold water and drain. Boil in slightly salted water until tender. Drain and retain the liquid. Preheat the oven to 400°F.

Heat the butter in a heavy pan and gently sauté the onion until transparent. Gradually stir in the flour. Slowly add the cauliflower liquid and half the grated cheese. Season to taste with salt and pepper, the herbs and mustard. Add more liquid in the form of hot water or vegetable stock to make a thick sauce. Put the cauliflower in a greased ovenproof dish and pour the sauce over. Sprinkle the nutmeg over and the rest of the cheese. Bake in the oven until the top is crisp and golden (15–25 minutes).

Baked Cauliflower
(Pain de Chou-fleur)

1 good-sized cauliflower
Salt
1 recipe white sauce (see under
Cabbage Loaf)

Freshly ground black pepper
2 eggs, beaten
3 tomatoes, sliced
1 tablespoon chopped parsley

Trim the cauliflower and cut into florets. Wash well in cold water and boil in slightly salted water until tender. Purée the cauliflower in a blender or food processor. Preheat the oven to 400°F.

Make the white sauce without adding cream to it and reduce it over a simmer until it is quite thick. In a bowl stir together the puréed cauliflower and the thick sauce. Season with salt and pepper to taste and add the beaten eggs. Put the mixture in a greased ovenproof dish and cover with some of the sliced tomato. Bake in the oven for 30 minutes. Turn out onto a serving dish and garnish with the rest of the tomato slices and chopped parsley.

Celeriac

This plant is a variety of celery which has a large edible root. It is this part of the plant which is used and it should always be firm when purchased.

Celeriac Salad
(*Salade de Céleri-rave*)

Serves 4

1 pound celeriac
Salt

1 tablespoon chopped capers

For the sauce:
²/₃ cup unsalted butter
3 egg yolks
Salt

Freshly ground white pepper
Juice of ½ lemon

Peel and trim the celeriac and cut into short, thin strips. Cook in boiling, slightly salted water for 1 minute. Remove and drain. Meanwhile make the Hollandaise sauce.

Melt the butter over low heat in a heavy pan. In another pan whisk the egg yolks and 2 tablespoons of water with a little salt and pepper to taste for half a minute. Put over low heat and remove the butter. Continue whisking until the mixture is creamy and the whisk begins to leave a trail. Remove from the heat. Slowly add the melted butter to the egg mixture a few drops at a time. Once the butter has been added, check the seasoning and add lemon juice to taste. Stir in the capers and pour over the celeriac in a serving dish.

Celeriac Purée

(Purée de Céleri-rave)

Serves 4

1 pound celeriac
½ pound potatoes
Salt
2 tablespoons butter

2 tablespoons heavy cream
Freshly ground pepper
Pinch nutmeg
1 teaspoon chopped mint

Peel and trim the celeriac and cut in pieces. Boil in water until tender. Drain. Boil the potatoes in slightly salted water until tender. Drain and peel. Put both vegetables in a blender or food processor and purée. Put in a serving dish and stir in the butter, cream, salt and pepper to taste and nutmeg. Garnish with the chopped mint.

Celeriac Patties

(Croquettes de Céleri-rave)

Serves 4–6

1 pound celeriac
Salt
1 pound potatoes
3 egg yolks
Freshly ground black pepper

Pinch freshly grated nutmeg
1 teaspoon chopped parsley
Whole wheat flour
Oil for deep-frying
Lemon wedges

Peel and trim the celeriac and cut into pieces. Boil in slightly salted water until tender. Drain and mash. Boil the potatoes in slightly salted water until soft. Peel and mash. Mix the celeriac and potato in a bowl with the egg yolks, seasoning and parsley. Squeeze together to make walnut-sized balls. Roll in flour and flatten slightly. Deep-fry in hot oil until golden on both sides. Serve with lemon wedges.

Celeriac Fritters
(*Beignets de Céleri-rave*)

¾ pound celeriac
Salt
2 tablespoons whole wheat flour
3 tablespoons whole wheat
  breadcrumbs

1 egg, beaten
2 tablespoons melted butter
2 tablespoons olive oil

For the sauce:
½ cup chopped walnuts
3 tablespoons butter
2 tablespoons grated parmesan
  cheese
1 clove garlic

2 tablespoons heavy cream
Salt
Freshly ground black pepper
Vegetable stock

Peel and trim the celeriac and cut into strips as for Celeriac Salad. Boil in slightly salted water for 10 minutes. Drain. Mix the flour with the breadcrumbs. Put the beaten egg in a bowl and put in the celeriac strips so that they are well coated with egg. Roll in the flour and breadcrumb mixture. Heat the butter and oil in a heavy frying pan and fry the celeriac strips until just golden. Keep warm.

Make the sauce by pounding the nuts, butter, cheese and garlic to make a thick paste. Stir in the cream and season with salt and pepper to taste. Put in a pan and heat gently. Gradually add stock until a sauce is made of the desired consistency. Serve with the celeriac strips.

Celery

Although introduced by the Romans, celery was not widely cultivated in France until the sixteenth century. The Loire valley is the principal region of production. Make sure the stalks are always firm and crisp. Celery is sold in France with the leaves intact and they make an excellent flavoring herb.

Celery with Herbs
(*Céleri en Branche aux Fines Herbes*)   Serves 4

2 heads celery
Salt
Butter
Bunch chopped fresh tarragon
2 teaspoons chopped marjoram
½ cup vegetable stock
½ cup dry wine

Freshly ground black pepper
3 tablespoons whole wheat
  breadcrumbs
3 tablespoons crème fraîche *or*
  natural yogurt
1 teaspoon chopped parsley

Trim the celery and cut the stalks into large pieces. Cook in boiling, slightly salted water until just tender. Drain. Put in a well-buttered ovenproof dish. Preheat the oven to 350°F.

Put the tarragon and marjoram in a small heavy pan and pour the stock and wine over. Season with salt and pepper to taste and heat gently for 10 minutes. Pour over the celery. Sprinkle the breadcrumbs over and spread with the crème fraîche. Bake in the oven until the top begins to turn golden (20–30 minutes). Serve sprinkled with chopped parsley.

Celery with Tomatoes
(*Céleri aux Tomates*)   Serves 4

3 tablespoons melted butter
1 tablespoon olive oil
1 onion, finely chopped
1¼ cups chopped tomatoes
1 head celery
1 teaspoon chopped thyme

1 teaspoon chopped basil
Salt
Freshly ground black pepper
1 cup vegetable stock
½ cup red wine
2 teaspoons chopped parsley

Heat the butter in a heavy pan with the olive oil. Gently sauté the onion until transparent. Add the tomatoes and turn in the oil. Trim the celery and cut into pieces. Add to the tomatoes with the herbs, salt and pepper to taste. Stir together and add the stock and wine. Cover and simmer until the celery is tender (about 5 minutes). Serve garnished with chopped parsley.

Braised Celery
(*Céleri Braisé*)   Serves 4

2 heads celery
Salt
1 onion, finely chopped
3 tablespoons melted butter
1 tablespoon olive oil

2 tablespoons whole wheat flour
1 cup vegetable stock
1 cup dry wine
Freshly ground black pepper

Trim the celery and cut into pieces. Blanch in slightly salted, boiling water for 2 minutes. Drain. Put the onion in a heavy pan with the butter and olive oil and gently sauté until the onion just begins to turn golden. Stir in the flour and add the celery pieces. Turn well in the *roux*. Gradually add the stock and wine. Season with salt and pepper to taste. Cook together until the celery is just tender (a few minutes).

Celery Salad
(*Salade de Céleri*)

Serves 4

1 head celery
Juice of half lemon

Mayonnaise (see recipe under
  Cauliflower Salad)

Wash and trim the celery. Slice and put in a bowl. Sprinkle with lemon juice and leave to stand while you prepare the mayonnaise. Check the seasonings, adding more mustard, salt and pepper if desired. Add enough of the mayonnaise to coat the celery and mix well. Cover with a cloth and let stand for 1 hour before serving.

Celery with Chestnuts
(*Céleri en Branche aux Marrons*)

Serves 4

1 head celery
Lemon juice
1 pound chestnuts
2 tablespoons melted butter

Salt
Freshly ground black pepper
Vegetable stock

Trim the celery, cut into pieces; keep some of the green leaf for garnish. Put in a bowl and sprinkle with lemon juice. Put the chestnuts in a pan after slitting each with a knife. Cover with water and boil for 10 minutes. Drain and peel. Put the butter in a heavy pan and add the peeled chestnuts. Heat gently and turn the chestnuts in the butter. Season with salt and pepper to taste and pour in enough stock to just cover. Put the lid on the pan and simmer gently for 5 minutes. Add the celery pieces. Make sure there is enough stock to just cover the chestnuts and celery, adding more if necessary. Continue simmering until the chestnuts are tender. Serve garnished with a little chopped celery leaf.

This dish also goes well with a white sauce (see under the recipe for Cabbage Loaf).

Celery Soup
(*Potage au Céleri*)

2 tablespoons melted butter
1 onion, finely chopped
½ pound potatoes, chopped
1 pound celery, trimmed and
  chopped

Salt
Freshly ground pepper
6 cups warm water
1 teaspoon celery seed (optional)
¼ cup heavy cream

Heat the butter in a heavy soup pot and gently sauté the onion until transparent. Add the potatoes and celery. Keep a little of the celery leaf as a garnish. Add salt and pepper to taste and the water and celery seed. Cook the celery and potato until both vegetables are tender. Purée in a blender or food processor. Put back in the pan and add the cream. Heat gently but do not allow to boil.

Chestnuts

Chestnuts are used in many parts of France as a vegetable, especially where they are plentiful, as in the regions of Poitou and Limousin. To prepare them for cooking, make a slit in the shell with a knife and place in a pan of cold water. Bring to a boil and allow to simmer for 5 minutes. Drain and cool under cold water. Now the shell and skin can be removed with a sharp knife.

Braised Chestnuts
(*Marrons Braisés*)   Serves 4–6

2 pounds chestnuts
2 stalks celery, chopped
1 teaspoon brown sugar

¼ cup (½ stick) butter
Salt
Freshly ground black pepper

Prepare the chestnuts for cooking as described above. Put in a heavy pan with the celery, sugar and butter. Season with salt and pepper. Pour in enough water to just cover. Bring to a boil and simmer together until the chestnuts are tender (about 30 minutes). Raise the heat at the end to allow the excess liquid to evaporate. Remove the celery before serving.

To make chestnut purée, cook the chestnuts in milk or stock with the rest of the ingredients. Remove the celery and purée the chestnuts in a food processor or put through a food mill. Beat in a little more melted butter before serving.

Chick Peas

There are many varieties of this Mediterranean legume, one of which is cultivated in France. Soak dried chick peas in water the day before they are needed. Next day change the water and boil for 10 minutes. Drain and continue boiling in fresh water until the chick peas are tender. Canned chick peas may also be used, in which case no pre-boiling is necessary.

Chick Pea Salad
(Salade de Pois Chiches)   Serves 4

2 cups chick peas, cooked with a
   bay leaf and a few cloves
Olive oil
Wine vinegar

Salt
Freshly ground black pepper
Sliced scallions
Chopped parsley

Arrange the chick peas in a serving dish and serve with the rest of the ingredients to taste. People can have individual servings of peas and make up their own dressings. Lemon juice may be substituted for the wine vinegar. Other herbs such as fresh tarragon may be added to the dish as desired.

Chick Pea and Spinach Bake
(*Gratin de Pois Chiches aux Épinards*) Serves 6

2 pounds fresh spinach
Salt
4 tablespoons olive oil
1 small onion, finely chopped
1¼ cups chopped tomatoes
2-4 cloves garlic, finely chopped
2 teaspoons chopped basil
1 teaspoon chopped savory

Freshly ground black pepper
1¼ cups cooked chick peas
2 hard-boiled eggs
A few sage leaves
3 tablespoons whole wheat
   breadcrumbs
2 tablespoons melted butter

Trim the spinach and boil in slightly salted water for 3 minutes. Drain and chop. Preheat the oven to 400°F.

Heat the olive oil in a heavy pan and gently sauté the onion until transparent. Add the tomatoes and sauté together until the tomatoes soften. Add the garlic, herbs, salt and pepper to taste. Cook together for 5 minutes. Mix the chick peas with the tomatoes. Chop the eggs in a bowl and stir in the spinach and sage leaves. Stir into the tomato and chick peas and put the mixture in a greased ovenproof dish. Cover with the breadcrumbs and dribble the melted butter over. Bake in the oven until the top is crisp and golden (20–30 minutes).

Chick Peas with Tomatoes
(*Pois Chiches aux Tomates*) Serves 4

4 tablespoons olive oil
1 onion, finely chopped
2¼ cups chopped tomatoes
2 cups cooked chick peas
2-4 cloves garlic, finely chopped
1 teaspoon chopped sage
1 teaspoon chopped basil

1 teaspoon chopped thyme
Salt
Freshly ground black pepper
½ cup red wine
½ cup vegetable stock
1 tablespoon chopped parsley

Heat the oil in a heavy pan and sauté the onion until it just begins to turn golden. Add the tomatoes and turn in the oil for 5 minutes. Add the chick peas, garlic, herbs, salt and pepper to taste and turn in the oil. Add the wine and stock. Cover and cook together for 10 minutes. Serve garnished with chopped parsley.

Cucumber

Cucumber Salad
(*Salade de Concombres*)

Serves 4

1 large cucumber, sliced
½ cup natural yogurt
2 tablespoons fresh chives *or*
    mint

Salt
Freshly ground black pepper

Put the cucumber in a salad bowl with the yogurt and 1 tablespoon of the herbs. Season with salt and pepper to taste. Mix together well. Garnish with the remaining herbs and serve chilled.

Cucumber with Cream Sauce
(*Concombre à la Crème*)

Serves 4

1 pound large *or* small
    cucumbers
4 tablespoons melted butter
1 cup heavy cream *or* natural
    yogurt

1 cup vegetable stock
Salt
Freshly ground black pepper
1 tablespoon chopped chives

Wash the cucumber and slice (lengthwise if the cucumbers are small). Heat the butter in a heavy pan and gently sauté the cucumber for 2 minutes, turning the slices in the hot butter all the time. Pour in the cream, stock and sprinkle with salt and pepper to taste. Cook together over low heat and do not allow to boil. When the cucumber is just tender, serve garnished with the chopped chives.

Cucumber Summer Soup
(*Potage Glacé au Concombre*)

Serves 4

1 cucumber
2 cloves garlic
2 cups natural yogurt
1 cup vegetable stock
1 cup dry white wine

Salt
Freshly ground black pepper
1 sprig tarragon
1 teaspoon finely chopped
  parsley

Wash the cucumber and put a few slices on one side to garnish the soup later. Chop the cucumber and purée in a blender or food processor with the garlic. Put in a soup pot with the yogurt, stock and wine and heat through gently. Season with salt and pepper to taste. Allow to cool after a few minutes then chill. Serve chilled and garnished with the cucumber slices and herbs.

Cucumber with Herbs
(*Concombre aux Fines Herbes*)

Serves 4

1 cucumber
Salt
Freshly ground black pepper
Vegetable stock

1 teaspoon chopped basil
1 teaspoon chopped mint
2 tablespoons melted butter
1 tablespoon chopped parsley

Wash the cucumber and cut into short strips or chop. Put in a shallow pan and sprinkle with salt and pepper. Pour in enough stock to just cover the cucumber pieces. Sprinkle on the basil and mint and cover. Stew the dish gently for a few minutes until the cucumber is just tender. Pour off any excess liquid and put in a serving dish. Spread the butter over and serve garnished with the parsley.

Eggplant

Eggplant has been cultivated in France since the beginning of the seventeenth century, especially in the warm south where it is an important vegetable in the southern cuisine. It is also known in France as *melongena* and *morelle*.

Eggplant with Cream Sauce
(*Aubergines à la Crème*)   Serves 4

1 pound eggplant
Salt
6 tablespoons olive oil
2 cloves garlic, finely chopped
1 cup natural yogurt

1 cup heavy cream
1 tablespoon chopped parsley
Freshly ground black pepper
1 teaspoon chopped mint

Trim the eggplant and cut into slices. Sprinkle with salt and leave in a colander to drain for 30 minutes. Wash in cold water and dry. Heat the olive oil in a heavy pan and gently sauté the eggplant slices until they are golden on both sides. Allow to drain. In another pan, use a little of the hot oil to sauté the garlic for 2 minutes. Add the yogurt, cream, parsley and salt and pepper to taste. Allow to heat through but do not allow the sauce to boil. Put the eggplant slices on a serving dish and pour the sauce over. Sprinkle with the chopped mint.

Eggplant Charlotte
(*Charlotte d'Aubergines*)

Serves 6

The word *charlotte* entered the English language as a culinary term in the nineteenth century and is usually thought of as a dessert. Here it is a delicious savory dish.

2 pounds eggplant	Freshly ground black pepper
Salt	1 teaspoon chopped basil
1 cup olive oil	1 teaspoon chopped parsley
1 onion, finely chopped	1 cup natural yogurt
2–4 cloves garlic, finely chopped	1 cup vegetable stock
2 pounds ripe tomatoes	

Wash and trim the eggplant. Cut into thick slices, sprinkle with salt and leave to drain in a colander for 30 minutes. Wash with cold water and allow to dry. Heat 2 tablespoons of oil in a frying pan and gently sauté the onion until it just begins to turn golden. Add the garlic, tomatoes, salt and pepper to taste and the herbs. Simmer together for 20 minutes. Put one-third of the tomato mixture on one side to make a sauce.

In another pan sauté the eggplant slices in the rest of the oil until golden on both sides. Add more oil if necessary. Preheat the oven to 350°F.

Put a layer of eggplant slices in a 4 cup charlotte mold or pudding mold. Arrange the slices so that they also overlap around the edge of the mold. Spread with some of the tomato mixture and some of the yogurt. Continue making these layers until the eggplant slices and the yogurt are used up. Finish with a layer of eggplant slices. Cover the mold with aluminum foil and bake in the oven for 45 minutes. Allow to cool a little before upending it onto a serving dish. The charlotte should come out in one piece. Put the stock in a saucepan and add the remaining tomato mixture. Stir together over a simmer. Spoon the sauce around the edge of the charlotte and serve the rest with slices of the dish.

Eggplant Stew
(*Ratatouille*)   Serves 4

This is the classic vegetable stew from Provence. It should always feature the soft vegetables and tangy herbs from southern France.

1 medium eggplant
½ pound zucchini, sliced
½ pound pumpkin, cubed
4 tablespoons olive oil
2 medium onions, sliced
4 large tomatoes, chopped
2 red *or* green peppers, seeded and sliced
6-10 black olives, pitted and halved (optional)

2-4 cloves garlic, crushed *or* finely chopped
1 teaspoon chopped basil
1 teaspoon chopped thyme
½ teaspoon ground coriander seeds
Pinch ground aniseed
Salt
Freshly ground black pepper
1 tablespoon chopped parsley

Slice the eggplant lengthwise and cut each half into slices. Sprinkle the eggplant and zucchini slices with a little water and leave to drain in a colander for 20-30 minutes. Heat 2 tablespoons of the oil in a large pan or casserole and gently sauté the onions until they soften. Add the drained eggplant, zucchini, tomatoes, peppers, olives, garlic, herbs and salt and pepper to taste. Mix together well and sprinkle the rest of the oil over. Cover and simmer gently until all the vegetables are tender. Stir in the chopped parsley just before serving.

Baked Eggplant
(*Aubergines au Four*)   Serves 6

2 pounds eggplant
Salt
4-6 tablespoons olive oil
2 pounds tomatoes, chopped
4 cloves garlic, finely chopped
Freshly ground black pepper

1 teaspoon chopped thyme
1 teaspoon chopped basil
1 teaspoon chopped marjoram
1 cup grated gruyère *or* cheddar cheese

Trim the eggplant and cut into thick slices. Sprinkle with a little salt and let drain in a colander. Wash with cold water and dry. Preheat the oven to 400°F.

Heat the oil in a frying pan and sauté the eggplant slices until they are golden on both sides. Put on one side to drain on paper towels. Put in the tomatoes once all the eggplant slices have been cooked and sauté for 2 minutes. Add the garlic, salt and pepper to taste and herbs. Cook together for 10 minutes. Put half of the mixture into an ovenproof dish. Arrange the eggplant slices over this. Sprinkle with half of the cheese. Pour the rest of the tomato mixture over and cover with the rest of the cheese. Bake in the oven until the top is nice and golden (30–45 minutes).

Eggplant Fritters
(*Beignets d'Aubergines*)   Serves 4

½ cup whole wheat flour
Salt
2 teaspoons olive oil
1 egg white
1 pound eggplant

Oil for deep-frying
Lemon slices
Black olives
Sprig of parsley

To make the batter, sift the flour and a pinch of salt together in a bowl. Make a well in the center and pour in the oil and 3 tablespoons of lukewarm water. Gradually mix with the flour until a smooth, creamy batter is formed, adding another 2 or 3 tablespoons of water if needed. Leave to one side for 30 minutes. Just before the batter is needed, whip the egg white well and fold into the batter. Mix well.

Meanwhile, slice the eggplant, sprinkle with a little salt and allow to drain in a colander for 30 minutes. When the slices are ready, heat the oil in a heavy pan. Bring the batter near. When the oil is hot, dip slices of eggplant in the batter and fry in the hot oil until golden. Allow to drain and arrange on a serving dish with slices of lemon and olives. Garnish with a sprig of parsley. Serve hot or cold.

Eggplant Midi-Style
(Aubergines au Midi) Serves 4

In France, the south is known as the Midi. The warm climate and long summers are particularly conducive to growing the soft vegetables such as eggplant and zucchini.

1 pound eggplant
1 pound zucchini
Salt
Oil for frying
¼ cup (½ stick) butter
3 cups chopped mushrooms
1 onion, chopped

2 cloves garlic, finely chopped
4 tablespoons whole wheat
  breadcrumbs
Freshly ground black pepper
1 teaspoon chopped oregano
1 teaspoon chopped thyme

Slice the eggplant and zucchini thickly and sprinkle with a little salt. Allow to drain in a colander for 30 minutes. Heat 6 tablespoons of oil in a heavy pan and sauté the eggplant and zucchini slices until just golden on each side, adding more oil as necessary. Keep warm to one side.

Melt the butter in another pan and gently sauté the mushrooms for 5 minutes. Remove and keep warm. Put in the onion, adding more oil if necessary and sauté until just golden. Add the garlic, breadcrumbs, salt and pepper to taste and the herbs. Cook together for 5 minutes. Stir in the mushrooms. Arrange the eggplant and zucchini slices on a serving dish and cover with the mushroom mixture. Serve hot.

Eggplant Provence-Style
(Aubergines à la Provençale) Serves 6

2 pounds eggplant
Salt
Oil for frying
4 eggs, beaten
2–4 cloves garlic

1 teaspoon chopped parsley
1 teaspoon chopped thyme
Freshly ground black pepper
¾ cup grated gruyère *or* cheddar
  cheese

Slice the eggplant, sprinkle with a little salt and leave to drain in a colander. Heat 6 tablespoons of oil in a heavy pan and fry the eggplant slices until just golden on both sides, adding more oil if necessary. Allow to drain. Preheat the oven to 400°F.

Reduce the eggplant to a purée in a blender or food processor and pour into a bowl. Stir in the eggs. Crush the garlic well and add the herbs and salt and pepper to taste. Pour the mixture into a greased ovenproof dish and bake in the oven until the eggs are set on top (about 10 minutes). Sprinkle with cheese, lower the heat to 350°F and bake until the top is golden (20–30 minutes).

Endive

Chicory is known in Belgium as *chicorée de Bruxelles* and in the United States as endive. It is a tight-leaved vegetable with a pale center and dark outer leaves.

Endive Gratin
(Endives au Gratin)   Serves 4

1½ pounds endive
Butter
Salt
Freshly ground black pepper
3 tablespoons grated parmesan
  cheese
3 tablespoons whole wheat
  breadcrumbs

1 tablespoon chopped parsley
2 tablespoons olive oil *or* melted
  butter
3 tablespoons crème fraîche *or*
  heavy cream
½ teaspoon paprika

Trim the endive and split the heads in half lengthwise. Put with the split side down in a well-buttered, ovenproof dish. Preheat the oven to 400°F. Sprinkle the endive with salt and pepper. Mix the cheese, breadcrumbs and parsley together in a bowl. Spread over the endive. Trickle olive oil over the top and bake in the oven for 10 minutes. Turn down the heat to 350°F. After 10 minutes, spread the crème fraîche over the top and sprinkle on the paprika. Continue baking until the chicory is tender (30–40 minutes).

Endive Salad
(*Salade d'Endives*)

½ pound endive
½ pound red-skinned apples
2 cups small mushrooms
¾ cup natural yogurt *or* crème
   fraîche

Salt
Freshly ground black pepper
Handful chopped walnuts
½ cup cooked chopped beets
Lemon juice

Trim the endive and cut into thick slices. Core the apples and cut into small chunks. Slice the mushrooms. Put the endive, apples and mushrooms into a salad bowl. In a separate bowl mix together the yogurt, salt and pepper to taste and the walnuts. Pour over the salad vegetables and mix together. Sprinkle the chopped beets over the salad. Sprinkle with lemon juice to taste.

Braised Endive
(*Endives Braisées*)

Serves 4

1½ pounds endive
2 tablespoons melted butter
Salt
Freshly ground black pepper

1 teaspoon soft brown sugar
1 tablespoon lemon juice
1 tablespoon chopped parsley

Preheat the oven to 350°F. Trim the endive heads. Spread the bottom and sides of an ovenproof dish with butter. Put in the endive. Sprinkle with salt, pepper, sugar, lemon juice and 2 tablespoons of water. Cover the dish with a piece of aluminum foil and bake in the oven until the endive is tender inside (50–60 minutes). Serve garnished with the chopped parsley.

Endive with Cream Sauce
(Endives à la Crème)

Serves 4

1½ pounds endive
2 tablespoons melted butter
Salt
Freshly ground black pepper
1 teaspoon soft brown sugar
1 tablespoon lemon juice

1 cup heavy cream
½ cup vegetable stock
2 tablespoons dry white wine
Lemon slices
2 teaspoons chopped parsley

Prepare the endive as in the previous recipe for Braised Endive. Meanwhile gently heat the cream, stock and wine together in a heavy pan. Do not allow to boil. Season with salt and pepper to taste. When the endive is cooked, pour the cream sauce over and serve garnished with lemon slices and chopped parsley.

Fava Beans

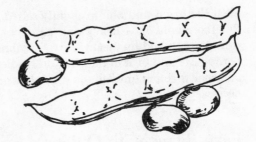

Fava Beans Touraine-Style
(*Fèves à la Tourangelle*)

Serves 6

A wine from the Loire valley will give the authentic taste to the sauce.

3 pounds fava beans
¼ cup (½ stick) butter
A few sage leaves
2 teaspoons chopped savory
2 cups dry white wine

Salt
Freshly ground black pepper
2 tablespoons crème fraîche *or* natural yogurt
1 tablespoon chopped chives

Shell the beans. Heat the butter in a heavy pan. Add the beans and herbs and turn in the butter for 5 minutes. Add the wine. Add salt and pepper to taste and simmer together for 10 minutes. Add the crème fraîche and cook together until the beans are tender. Serve garnished with the chopped chives.

Fava Bean Stew
(*Ragoût de Fèves*)

Serves 6

3 pounds fava beans
Salt
2 onions, chopped
3 tablespoons olive oil
1 tablespoon melted butter
1¼ cups sliced carrots
2 cups shredded young cabbage

1¼ cups chopped tomatoes
Freshly ground black pepper
2 teaspoons chopped parsley
2 teaspoons chopped sage
1 cup water *or* vegetable stock
1 cup red wine

Shell the beans and boil in slightly salted water for 5 minutes. Drain. Put the onions in a heavy pan and cook in the oil and butter until transparent. Add the beans, carrots, cabbage, tomatoes, salt and pepper to taste and turn in the oil. Add the herbs, stock or water and wine and cook together until all the vegetables are tender. Add more liquid as necessary.

Fava Beans with Onions
(*Fèves aux Ciboules*)   Serves 4

2 pounds fava beans	1 bunch scallions, chopped
Salt	1 clove garlic, crushed
A few sage leaves	Freshly ground black pepper
3 tablespoons melted butter	2 teaspoons chopped savory

Shell the beans and cook in slightly salted water with the sage leaves until tender. Drain and retain the liquid. Keep the beans warm. In a heavy pan, heat the butter and gently sauté the scallions until transparent. Add the garlic, salt and pepper to taste, savory and the cooked beans. Stir together and add any of the retained liquid to make a sauce. When the garlic is well cooked, serve hot.

Creamed Fava Beans
(*Fèves à la Crème*)   Serves 4

2 pounds fava beans	2 egg yolks
Salt	Salt
1 teaspoon soft brown sugar	Freshly ground black pepper
2 tablespoons natural yogurt	1 teaspoon chopped sage
½ cup heavy cream	1 teaspoon chopped savory

Shell the beans and put in a pan with water to just cover. Add salt and sugar and boil until the beans are tender. Drain and retain the liquid. In a heavy pan gently heat the yogurt, cream, egg yolks, salt and pepper to taste and herbs. Stir together but do not allow to boil. Add any of the bean liquid if you want the sauce to be thinner. Put the beans on a serving dish and pour the cream sauce over.

Fava Beans with Lettuce
(*Fèves à la Laitue*)

Serves 6

2 tablespoons melted butter
1 tablespoon olive oil
1 onion, finely chopped
3 pounds fava beans
2 cups water
1 teaspoon soft brown sugar

Salt
Freshly ground black pepper
2 teaspoons chopped sage
2 teaspoons chopped savory
½ iceberg lettuce, shredded

Heat the butter and oil in a heavy pan and gently sauté the onion until transparent. Shell the beans and add to the pan. Turn in the oil for 5 minutes. Add the water, sugar, salt and pepper to taste and the herbs. Cover and cook together for 10 minutes. Put in the lettuce and continue cooking until the beans are tender. Serve hot.

Fava Bean Soup
(*Potage aux Fèves*)

Serves 6

2 tablespoons olive oil *or* melted
    butter
1 small bunch scallions, chopped
1½ pounds fresh fava beans
7½ cups water

Salt
Freshly ground black pepper
2 tablespoons melted butter
2 egg yolks

Heat the oil in a heavy soup pot and gently sauté the scallions until transparent. Add the shelled beans and turn in the oil for 2 minutes. Add the water and salt and pepper to taste. Simmer until the beans are tender. Drain off the liquid and retain. Purée the beans in a food processor or blender. Put the puréed beans and the retained liquid in the soup pot and warm through. Stir in the butter and egg yolks. Do not allow the soup to boil.

This soup is delicious with chunky bread and a little grated cheese.

Fennel

This member of the umbel family includes parsley and coriander and is of Italian origin. It is now widely cultivated, especially in the south, and the bulbous stem and leaves are used as a vegetable. It has a slight flavor of aniseed.

Fennel Provence-Style
(*Fenouil à la Provençale*)

Serves 4

This combination of garlic, herbs and a robust dry wine, such as a Côtes de Provence, produces a taste that is typically Provençale.

4 small heads fennel
Salt
4 tablespoons olive oil
1 onion, finely chopped
1¼ cups chopped tomatoes
2–4 cloves garlic, finely chopped

2 teaspoons chopped basil
1 teaspoon chopped oregano
Freshly ground black pepper
1 cup vegetable stock
1 cup dry wine
A few black olives, pitted

Trim the fennel and blanch in slightly salted, boiling water for 15 minutes. Drain and rinse under cold water. Drain again and cut each bulb into quarters. Heat the oil in a heavy pan and gently sauté the onion until it begins to turn golden. Add the tomatoes, garlic, herbs and salt and pepper to taste. Turn in the oil for 5 minutes. Put in the fennel quarters and the rest of the ingredients. Cover and cook over low heat 15 minutes longer.

Fennel Salad
(*Salade de Fenouil*)

Serves 4

2 medium fennel bulbs
Salt
1 tablespoon wine vinegar
Freshly ground black pepper

½ teaspoon Dijon mustard
3 tablespoons olive oil
½–1 clove garlic, finely chopped

Trim and slice the fennel bulbs. Blanch in slightly salted, boiling water for 2 minutes. Drain well. Make up the vinaigrette by whisking together the vinegar, a pinch of salt and pepper and the mustard. Gradually whisk in the oil and garlic until the sauce is well blended. Toss the fennel with the vinaigrette in a salad bowl. Cover with a cloth and allow to stand for 1 hour before serving.

Pickled Fennel Salad
(*Fenouil à la Grecque*)

Serves 4–6

2 cups water
½ cup olive oil
Juice of 1 lemon
1 pound fennel
1 teaspoon fennel seeds

1 sprig parsley
1 sprig tarragon
Salt
Freshly ground black pepper

Mix the water, olive oil and lemon juice together in a pan. Make sure that the pan is not affected by acids. Trim the fennel and slice thinly. Put the green leaf in with the marinade mixture and keep the slices to one side. Add the herbs and salt and pepper to taste to the marinade. Heat the marinade gently for 5 minutes. Put in the fennel slices and continue heating together for a further 5 minutes. Remove the herb sprigs and allow the fennel to cool in the marinade overnight. Drain off most of the marinade before serving.

Fennel Soup
(*Potage au Fenouil*)

Serves 4–6

2 tablespoons butter
2 tablespoons olive oil
2 heads fennel, trimmed and
  finely sliced
½ pound potatoes, chopped
1 stalk celery, sliced
1 clove garlic, finely chopped

6 cups vegetable stock
1 cup natural yogurt *or* crème
  fraîche
Salt
Freshly ground black pepper
Fennel leaves and celery leaves,
  for garnish

Heat the butter and oil in a heavy soup pot and gently sauté the fennel for 3 minutes. Add the potatoes and celery and turn together in the oil for a further 5 minutes. Add the garlic and stock and simmer together for 20 minutes. Purée this mixture in a blender or food processor. Return to the soup pot and stir in the yogurt. Add seasoning to taste and gently heat through. Serve with sautéed or heated bread.

To garnish, use a few finely chopped fennel leaves and celery leaves.

Braised Fennel
(*Fenouils Braisés*)

Serves 4

4 heads fennel (not too large)
4 tablespoons butter
Salt
Freshly ground black pepper

1 teaspoon chopped chives
1 teaspoon chopped parsley
1 teaspoon chopped tarragon

Trim the fennel and save a little of the fresh leaves for a garnish. Blanch in slightly salted, boiling water for 15 minutes. Remove and rinse under cold water and allow to drain. Cut each bulb into quarters. Heat the butter in a heavy pan and gently braise the fennel quarters until they just begin to turn golden. Sprinkle with salt and pepper to taste and serve garnished with the chopped herbs, including the fresh fennel leaf.

Garlic

This excellent vegetable is the base of most of the southern-style cuisine, particularly the Provençale style. Well known for its health-promoting properties, it used to be carried by doctors in the sixteenth and seventeenth centuries as a guard against contracting infections.

Garlic Soup
(Soup à l'Ail)   Serves 4

4 tablespoons olive oil
1 large onion *or* 2 small leeks, sliced
1¼ cups chopped tomatoes
2 potatoes, chopped
4 cloves garlic, crushed

6 cups vegetable stock
½ cup wine
Salt
Freshly ground black pepper
1 teaspoon chopped basil
1 teaspoon chopped parsley

Heat the oil in a heavy soup pot and gently sauté the onion until just golden. Add the tomatoes, potatoes and garlic and turn in the oil for 5 minutes. Add the stock and the rest of the ingredients. Cover and cook for 20 minutes. Check the seasoning. Add more crushed garlic if needed.

Serve with sautéed or warm, crusty bread. This can be done southern-style by putting the bread in the soup bowl and pouring the soup over it.

Garlic and Walnut Dip
(Aïllade Toulousaine)

This relative of Aïoli comes from the walnut-growing regions of the Languedoc and Dordogne. Ideally fresh walnuts should be used, but the addition of walnut oil helps to make the authentic taste and aroma with any good walnuts. Use in the same way as Aïoli with raw or cooked vegetables and crusty bread.

4 cloves garlic
Pinch salt

3–4 tablespoons shelled walnuts
½ cup walnut oil *or* olive oil

Pound the garlic and salt, then add the walnuts and pound together until a smooth paste is formed. Gradually add the oil, pounding continuously to make a thick sauce. Use the same day.

Garlic Mayonnaise
(Aïoli)

In Provence, the last big meal before Lent used to be Aïoli. This is used as a garnish for a variety of cooked ingredients such as fennel, onions, carrots, string beans, artichokes, unskinned potatoes, hard-boiled eggs and herbs. Arrange them tastefully on a dish and serve with the garlic mayonnaise.

4–6 cloves garlic
1 egg yolk
Pinch salt

1 cup olive oil
Freshly ground black pepper
   (optional)

Pound the garlic and egg yolk together to make a paste. Season with salt. Gradually add the oil, drop by drop, pounding it into the paste. Season with pepper. Continue pounding until a smooth, thick mayonnaise is made.

Herbs

Since medieval times herbs have found a special place in European cooking. It has always been the custom both to collect wild herbs for culinary use as well as to grow them in the garden. Cultivated herbs for kitchen use are known as *fines herbes*. The collection of herbs known as *bouquet garni* consists of thyme, parsley, marjoram and basil wrapped in a cloth package. People vary both the ingredients and the quantities to make up the bouquet garni. Many cooks remove the herb package after it has served its purpose of aromatizing the ingredients of the dish. Herbs present a lovely range of plants with which to experiment for taste, aroma and color. Use the following recipes as a basis for your own variations.

Herb Salad
(*Salade Verte*)   Serves 4

1 pound lettuce and other salad
   greens such as dandelion
   leaves, endive, watercress,
   borage, sorrel or arugula
1 tablespoon wine vinegar *or*
   2 teaspoons lemon juice
Pinch salt
Freshly ground black pepper

½ teaspoon Dijon mustard
3 tablespoons olive oil
½–1 clove garlic, crushed
2 tablespoons chopped fresh
   herbs such as basil, parsley,
   chives, chervil, tarragon,
   marjoram or chopped fennel
   leaf

Wash the salad greens and tear in pieces. Dry thoroughly. Make the vinaigrette by whisking the vinegar with the salt, pepper and mustard. Gradually add the oil and garlic and whisk together until the sauce is well blended. Toss with the greens just before they are needed. Sprinkle with the chopped herbs. The vinaigrette may be adjusted to suit individual tastes.

Herb Soup
(*Potage aux Fines Herbes*)

Serves 4

½ cup chopped potatoes
6 cups vegetable stock
Salt
Freshly ground black pepper
3–4 tablespoons melted butter

2 cups chopped lettuce
2 cups chopped sorrel
2 cups chopped dandelion leaves
2 tablespoons chopped chives
1 tablespoon chopped parsley

Put the potatoes in a large soup pot with the stock. Season with salt and pepper to taste and bring to a boil. Cover and simmer over low heat until the potatoes are soft. Mash the potatoes to thicken the stock. In a separate pan heat the butter and add the lettuce, sorrel, dandelion, chives and parsley. Turn in the butter over low heat for 3 minutes. Pour into the soup pot and heat together. Check the seasoning and serve hot with sautéed or warm bread.

Basil

Basil was once considered a royal plant and only the sovereign (*basileus*) was allowed to cut it. This was done with a golden sickle. The aromatic leaves are an essential ingredient in the Provençal flavoring *pistou*.

Basil and Garlic Soup
(*Soupe au Pistou*)

Serves 6

Pistou is the French relative of the Genovese *pesto* which also includes pounded pine nuts. Since the pounded pomade may be added to the soup just before consumption, it can add fun to a meal where each guest can help themselves from the communal bowl. This recipe is ideal for using up any vegetables that are at hand as well as any broken pasta that you are wondering what to do with.

3 tablespoons olive oil
1 onion, sliced
1 cup chopped carrots
2 cups chopped potatoes
2 cups chopped pumpkin
2 leeks, trimmed and sliced
1 pound navy beans
1 cup fava beans
2 teaspoons chopped thyme

2 teaspoons chopped marjoram
1 tablespoon chopped parsley
Salt
Freshly ground black pepper
9 cups water
½ pound string beans, sliced
½ pound zucchini, sliced
1 cup broken pasta *or* macaroni

For the pistou:
4 cloves garlic
Good handful fresh basil

½–1 cup grated parmesan cheese
1 cup olive oil

Heat the oil in a large soup pot and gently sauté the onion until transparent. Add the carrots, potatoes, pumpkin, leeks, beans, herbs, salt and pepper to taste. Heat the water while you stir the vegetables in the oil. Pour in the water. Cover and simmer until the vegetables are just tender. Add the green beans, zucchini and pasta and cook together for 10 minutes.

While the soup is cooking make the pistou. Pound the garlic in a mortar with the basil until the herb is well pulped. Add a little cheese and pound together. Keep adding the cheese until all the cheese is used up. Now gradually add the oil the same way until a thick cream is formed. Add to the soup just before serving or put in the middle of the table for people to serve themselves. Serve the soup with chunky bread and perhaps a bowl of olives. This dish makes a meal by itself.

Basil and Tomato with Scrambled Eggs
(*Tomates au Basilic avec Oeufs Brouillés*)
Serves 4

4 tablespoons olive oil
2 tomatoes, chopped
2–3 cloves garlic, finely chopped
1 tablespoon chopped basil
1 tablespoon melted butter

8 eggs
Salt
Freshly ground black pepper
1 tablespoon chopped chives

Heat the oil in a heavy pan and gently sauté the tomatoes for 5 minutes. Add the garlic and basil and continue sautéing until the tomatoes are nicely softened. Add the butter to the eggs in a bowl and beat together. Pour into the tomato mixture and stir in with a fork. Sprinkle with salt and pepper to taste and continue stirring with the fork until the desired consistency is obtained. Serve each portion garnished with a little chopped chives.

Chervil

Chervil has been cultivated as an herb in France for many centuries. It should have stiff stems and a curly leaf. Do not use limp chervil.

Chervil and Scrambled Eggs
(*Cerfeuil aux Oeufs Brouillés*)
Serves 4

8 eggs
Salt
Freshly ground black pepper

2 tablespoons chopped chervil
⅓ cup butter

Whisk the eggs with salt and pepper to taste until slightly frothy. Beat in the chervil. Melt the butter in a heavy pan over low heat. Add the eggs and stir constantly with a wooden spoon until they begin to thicken. Cook as slowly as possible. Remove from the heat while the eggs are still moist. Serve on slices of toast or bread sautéed in oil.

Dandelion

Known in France as *pissenlit* because of its diuretic properties, dandelion has been a popular wild herb for many centuries. Larger dandelion leaf is often cultivated in gardens for use as an herb. Gather the leaves when young and not too dark green and bitter.

Dandelion and Egg Salad
(*Salade de Pissenlit aux Oeufs*)   Serves 4

1 pound dandelion leaves
1 clove garlic, finely chopped
2–4 eggs, hard-boiled
Salt

Freshly ground black pepper
Olive oil
Wine vinegar
2 tomatoes, sliced

Wash the dandelion leaves and dry well. Tear into pieces with the fingers and mix together with the garlic. Arrange in a salad bowl with the eggs, which can be sliced or cut in halves. Sprinkle with salt and pepper to taste. Serve with olive oil and vinegar to taste and garnish with tomato slices.

Dandelion with Cheese and Walnuts
(*Salade de Pissenlit au Roquefort*)

Serves 4

7 cups dandelion leaves
½ cup roquefort *or* other blue
  cheese
1 clove garlic, finely chopped
A few scallions, sliced fine
Salt

Freshly ground black pepper
2 tablespoons chopped walnuts
A few sage leaves
Olive oil *or* walnut oil
Wine vinegar *or* lemon juice

Wash the dandelion leaves and dry well. Arrange in a salad bowl and add the cheese, garlic and scallions and sprinkle with salt and pepper to taste. Add the nuts and sage leaves and allow to stand for 30 minutes. Serve with an oil and vinegar dressing to taste.

Sorrel

This hardy perennial herb was known in Asia before 300 B.C. It was known in France during the thirteenth century as one of the English herbs and still grows wild.

Sorrel Soup
(*Soupe à l'Oseille*)

Serves 4

½ pound young sorrel leaves
3 tablespoons melted butter
1 onion, sliced
1 pound potatoes, chopped

Salt
Freshly ground black pepper
6 cups vegetable stock
2 tablespoons chopped chives

Wash the sorrel leaves and remove any coarse stalks. Slice. Heat the butter in a heavy soup pot and gently sauté the onion until transparent. Add the potatoes and turn in the hot butter for 3 minutes. Add the sorrel and turn again for 2 minutes. Season with salt and pepper to taste and add the stock. Cover and cook over low heat until the potatoes are tender. Mash them to thicken the soup. Serve garnished with chopped chives and crusty bread.

Braised Sorrel
(Oseille Braisée)

Serves 4

1½ pounds young sorrel leaves
3 tablespoons melted butter
Salt

Freshly ground black pepper
Freshly grated nutmeg

Wash the sorrel leaves and remove any coarse stalks. Slice. Heat the butter in a heavy pan and gently sauté the sorrel until the leaves soften. Season with salt, pepper and nutmeg to taste. Serve with sautéed or warm crusty bread.

Sorrel Omelette
(Omelette à l'Oseille)

Serves 2

3 cups young sorrel leaves
Butter
Salt
Freshly ground black pepper

4 eggs, beaten
2 tablespoons crème fraîche or
   natural yogurt
Freshly grated nutmeg

Wash the sorrel and remove any coarse stalks. Slice. Heat 2 tablespoons of butter in a heavy pan and gently sauté the sorrel for 2 minutes. Season with salt and pepper. Remove from the heat. Coat the bottom of an omelette pan with melted butter and pour in the eggs. When they begin to solidify, stir the crème fraîche into the sorrel. Put in the middle of the omelette. Sprinkle on some grated nutmeg. Allow the omelette to thicken. Remove from the pan just before the egg is completely solid.

Sorrel with Cream Sauce
(Oseille à la Crème)

Serves 4

1½ pounds young sorrel leaves
Salt
3 tablespoons melted butter
Freshly grated nutmeg

½ cup heavy cream *or* créme
 fraîche
Sautéed cooked potatoes
1 tablespoon chopped parsley

Wash the sorrel and remove any coarse stalks. Blanch in boiling, slightly salted water for 5 minutes. Slice. Heat the butter in a heavy pan and add the drained sorrel. Turn in the hot butter for 2 minutes. Season with nutmeg and stir in the cream. Put in the middle of a serving dish. Surround with sautéed potatoes which are garnished with parsley.

Watercress

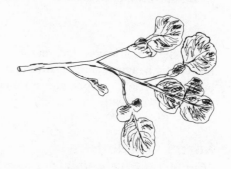

Watercress is such a strong-tasting herb that it is best prepared on its own without the addition of other herbs. Below is a simple country recipe that can be prepared in a few minutes.

Watercress with Cream
(Cresson à la Crème)

Serves 4

¾ pound watercress
3 tablespoons melted butter
Salt
Freshly ground black pepper
1 tablespoon dry wine

1 tablespoon vegetable stock
2 tablespoons crème fraîche *or*
 natural yogurt
2 tablespoons heavy cream

Wash the watercress and drain well. Heat the butter in a heavy pan and put in the watercress. Season with salt and pepper and turn in the hot butter for 3 minutes. Add the wine and stock, then the crème fraîche and cream. Cook together over low heat but do not allow the mixture to bubble. Serve after 2 minutes.

Watercress Soup
(*Potage au Cresson*)

Serves 4

1 large bunch watercress
3 tablespoons melted butter
Salt
Freshly ground black pepper
Freshly grated nutmeg
2 eggs

2 tablespoons grated parmesan
  cheese
6 cups vegetable stock
2 tablespoons grated gruyère *or*
  cheddar cheese

Wash the watercress well and chop. Heat the butter in a heavy soup pot and add the watercress. Turn in the hot butter for 3 minutes. Season with salt, pepper and nutmeg to taste. In a separate bowl, beat the eggs and beat in the cheese. Put the stock in the soup pot and bring to a boil. Add a cup of stock to the egg and cheese mixture. Stir together and add to the soup. Do not allow the soup to boil. Serve garnished with the cheese.

Leeks

Leek and Potato Soup
(Potage Fermière)

Serves 4–6

This soup is typical of the simple, substantial dishes which were prepared in the homes of farmers. Such dishes form the basis of good country cooking.

½ pound leeks
½ pound potatoes
½ pound carrots *or* parsnips
3 tablespoons butter
1 onion, finely chopped
6 cups water *or* vegetable stock

Salt
Freshly ground black pepper
½ cup heavy cream *or* yogurt
1 cup dry white wine (optional)
1 tablespoon finely chopped
parsley

Trim the leeks and wash well. Clean the potatoes and trim the carrots. Chop all the vegetables. Heat the butter in a heavy soup pot and gently sauté the onion until transparent. Add the chopped vegetables and turn in the butter for 3 minutes. Add the stock and season with salt and pepper to taste. Cover and simmer for 20 minutes. Remove from the heat and stir in the cream. Return to the heat but do not allow the dish to boil. If you have a cup of dry wine available this may be added to the soup also. Serve garnished with chopped parsley.

This soup may be puréed by passing through a blender or food processor before the cream is added.

Leek and Vegetable Soup
(*Potage aux Poireaux et Légumes*)

Serves 6

3 tablespoons olive oil
1 tablespoon melted butter
1 onion, finely chopped
2 good-sized leeks
¾ cup sliced string beans
2 carrots, sliced
2 stalks celery, sliced
½ cup chopped tomatoes
Salt

Freshly ground black pepper
2 bay leaves
1 teaspoon chopped oregano
1 teaspoon chopped marjoram
6 cups vegetable stock *or* water
½–1 cup dry wine
½ cup heavy cream
1 tablespoon finely chopped
   parsley *or* chervil

Heat the oil and butter in a heavy soup pot and gently sauté the onion until transparent. Add the leeks which have been trimmed, well washed and chopped and stir in the oil. Add the beans, carrots, celery and tomatoes. Season with salt and pepper to taste, bay leaf, oregano and marjoram. Turn in the oil for 3 minutes. Add the stock and wine. Cover and cook together until all the vegetables are well cooked. Serve hot with a little cream and chopped parsley on the top.

Leek Purée
(*Purée de Poireaux*)

Serves 6

2½ pounds leeks
Salt
4 tablespoons melted butter
Freshly ground black pepper

½ cup heavy cream *or* natural
   yogurt
1 teaspoon chopped tarragon

Trim the leeks and wash well. Chop and put in a pan with just enough water to cover. Sprinkle with a little salt and boil until the leeks are just tender. Drain. The liquid may be used for stock or soup-making. Heat the butter in a heavy pan and turn the leeks in the hot butter for 2 minutes. Put in a blender or food processor and purée. Put in a serving dish and stir in the cream. Serve garnished with the chopped tarragon.

Leeks and Mushrooms with Cream Sauce
(*Poireaux à la Crème*)

1 pound leeks
Salt
2 tablespoons olive oil
2 tablespoons melted butter
3 cups chopped mushrooms
Freshly ground black pepper
1-2 cloves garlic, finely chopped

½ cup dry white wine
½ cup natural yogurt *or* crème
  fraîche
½ cup heavy cream
Pinch freshly grated nutmeg
1 teaspoon chopped chives *or*
  parsley

Trim the leeks and wash well. Chop and boil in slightly salted water until just tender. Drain and save the leek liquid. Heat the oil and butter in a heavy pan and gently sauté the chopped mushrooms for 2 minutes. Sprinkle with salt and pepper to taste and add the garlic. Sauté together for 3 minutes. Add the wine and yogurt and heat together until well blended. Add the cream and stir together. Add any of the leek liquid if needed to make a thin sauce. Put in the leeks and heat through but do not allow the sauce to boil. Put in a serving dish and sprinkle with grated nutmeg and chopped herbs.

Leeks Savoy-Style
(*Poireaux à la Savoyarde*)

Serves 4

Lying between the Rhône Valley and the Alpine borders of Switzerland and Italy is the old province of Savoie. Here, leeks are treated to a delicate aromatization with pepper, nutmeg, scallions and parsley.

1 pound leeks
2 stalks celery
Salt
¼ cup (½ stick) butter
4-6 scallions, sliced
Freshly ground black pepper
1 tablespoon chopped parsley

4 tablespoons whole wheat
  breadcrumbs
4 tablespoons grated gruyère *or*
  cheddar cheese
Freshly grated nutmeg
2 tablespoons olive oil

Trim the leeks and celery and wash well. Chop and boil the vegetables together in slightly salted water until the leeks are just tender. Preheat the oven to 400°F. Heat the butter in a separate pan and gently sauté the scallions for 3 minutes. Season with salt and pepper to taste. Add the drained leeks, parsley and half the breadcrumbs. Sauté together for 5 minutes. Put in a greased ovenproof dish. Mix together the rest of the breadcrumbs, cheese and nutmeg. Spread over the top of the leek mixture. Sprinkle with olive oil and bake in the oven until the top is crisp and golden (15–20 minutes).

Lentils

Lentil Purée
(*Purée de Lentilles*)

Serves 4–6

2 cups lentils
1 carrot, peeled and chopped
2 potatoes, chopped
1 onion, chopped
Salt
Freshly ground black pepper

2 bay leaves
1 teaspoon chopped marjoram
1 teaspoon chopped thyme
2 teaspoons chopped parsley
Lemon wedges

Wash the lentils and let soak in water while you prepare the vegetables. It is not necessary to soak lentils overnight. Drain the lentils and put in a pan with the prepared vegetables. Sprinkle with salt and pepper to taste and add the herbs. Cover with cold water and bring to a boil. Simmer together over low heat until all the vegetables are tender. Purée in a blender or food processor. Serve with lemon wedges and crusty bread.

Lentils with Spinach
(*Lentilles aux Épinards*)

Serves 4

2 cups lentils
2 tablespoons olive oil
2 tablespoons melted butter
1 onion, finely chopped
1¼ cups chopped tomatoes
Salt

Freshly ground black pepper
1 bay leaf
1 teaspoon chopped parsley
1 pound spinach
1–2 cloves garlic, finely chopped

Wash the lentils and let soak in cold water. Heat the oil and butter in a heavy pan and gently sauté the onion until it begins to turn golden. Add the tomatoes and turn in the oil for 3 minutes. Season with salt and pepper to taste and add the bay leaf and parsley. Stir together for a further 3 minutes. Drain the lentils and put in the pan with the tomato mixture. Cover with warm water and allow to cook until the lentils are almost tender, adding more water as necessary.

Wash the spinach and tear the leaves away from the thick stalks. Put in with the lentils. Add the garlic and allow to cook together until the spinach is tender (a few minutes).

Lentils with Mustard Sauce
(*Lentilles à la Dijonnaise*)   Serves 4

This dish takes its name from a particular type of Dijon mustard which is used. This is the spicy mustard with whole mustard grains.

1½ cups lentils
2 tablespoons olive oil
2 tablespoons melted butter
1 onion, sliced
1-2 cloves garlic, crushed
1¼ cups chopped tomatoes
1 tablespoon chopped parsley
Salt

Freshly ground black pepper
3 cups vegetable stock
1 cup dry red wine
1-2 tablespoons Dijon mustard
  (the grainy kind)
2 tablespoons crème fraîche *or*
  natural yogurt

Wash the lentils in plenty of cold water and drain. Heat the oil and butter in a heavy pan and gently sauté the onion until transparent. Add the garlic, tomatoes, parsley and salt and pepper to taste. Stir together for 5 minutes. Gradually add the stock, wine and lentils and cook over low heat until tender, adding more stock if necessary. Stir in half the mustard and taste. If a good mustard taste is preferred, add the rest. Stir in the crème fraîche and heat through. Do not allow the dish to boil.

Lettuce

Lettuce and Cheese Salad
(Salade aux Fromages de Chèvre)   Serves 4

1 iceberg lettuce
Good handful young dandelion
   leaves
Olive oil
Wine vinegar *or* lemon juice
Salt

Freshly ground black pepper
1 teaspoon Dijon mustard
Handful chopped fresh herbs
½ pound goat's milk cheese,
   sliced

Wash the lettuce and dandelion leaves and dry well. Arrange in a bowl.
Make up a vinaigrette by whisking together the oil, vinegar, salt,
pepper and mustard to taste. Just before the salad is needed, toss the
lettuce and dandelion with the vinaigrette. Sprinkle with the herbs and
arrange slices of goat's cheese on the salad.

Braised Lettuce
(Laitues Braisées)   Serves 4

4 small iceberg lettuces
Salt
2 tablespoons melted butter
1 medium onion, finely chopped
1 cup hot vegetable stock

1 teaspoon chopped marjoram
1 teaspoon chopped thyme
Freshly ground black pepper
Whole wheat flour

Preheat the oven to 375°F. Wash the lettuces and pull off any damaged outer leaves.

Put the lettuces head down in a pan of boiling, slightly salted water and blanch for 5 minutes. Remove and drain and cut each lettuce in halves or quarters. Heat the butter in a casserole and gently sauté the onion until it begins to turn golden. Put the drained lettuce pieces on top of the onion. Pour the stock over and sprinkle with the herbs and salt and pepper to taste. Cover and put in the oven for 30 minutes. Remove the lettuces, put on a serving dish and keep warm. Thicken the sauce over low heat by stirring in a teaspoon or two of flour. Pour over the lettuces.

Lettuce with Mushrooms
(*Laitues aux Champignons*)   Serves 4

4 small iceberg lettuces
Salt
2 tablespoons olive oil
1 tablespoon melted butter
1 onion, finely chopped
½ pound small mushrooms, sliced

Freshly ground black pepper
1–2 cloves garlic, finely chopped
½ cup dry wine
1 teaspoon chopped basil
1 teaspoon chopped parsley
2 tablespoons heavy cream *or* crème fraîche

Trim the lettuces and discard any damaged outer leaves. Wash well and put head down in a pan of boiling, slightly salted water. Blanch for 5 minutes and drain well. Cut into halves or quarters. Keep warm. Heat the oil and butter in a heavy pan and gently sauté the onion until transparent. Add the mushrooms and turn in the oil for 3 minutes. Add a little salt and pepper to season and the garlic. Sauté together for a further 3 minutes. Add the wine, herbs and cream and heat through. Do not allow the sauce to boil. Put the lettuces on a serving dish and pour the mushroom sauce over.

Buckwheat Crêpes with Lettuce and Cheese Sauce
(*Galettes de Sarrasin à la Laitue*)

Buckwheat is thought to have been introduced into France by the Crusaders, hence its name "Saracen." Its ground seeds make a dark, nourishing flour. In Brittany these crêpes are known as *galettes*.

For the crêpes:
1 egg
1 cup milk
½ teaspoon salt

1 cup buckwheat flour
Butter for cooking

For the filling:
1 large iceberg lettuce
2 eggs, beaten
½ cup natural yogurt
¼ cup roquefort *or* cheddar cheese, crumbled *or* grated
2 tablespoons heavy cream *or* crème fraîche

1 teaspoon Dijon mustard (the grainy kind)
Freshly ground black pepper
Chopped chives *or* parsley to garnish

Make the batter by beating together the egg, milk and salt. Gradually add the buckwheat flour and beat in until smooth. Let stand.

Wash the lettuce and chop. Make the sauce by mixing together the eggs, yogurt, cheese, cream and mustard in a heavy pan. Heat over a pan of boiling water until the sauce thickens. Season with pepper to taste and keep warm.

Make the crêpes by heating a little butter in a heavy pan. Pour off the excess. Add a spoonful of batter to cover the bottom of the pan. Allow the crêpe to brown on both sides. Turn out onto a plate.

Fill each crêpe with chopped lettuce and a little sauce. Roll up and arrange on a serving dish. Pour the rest of the sauce over and garnish with chopped herbs.

Mushrooms

As in all country cooking, wild fare is a welcome addition to the pot. If you are able to identify wild edible mushrooms correctly, by all means substitute them in any of the following dishes.

Mushroom Omelette
(*Omelette aux Champignons*)   Serves 2

4 eggs
Salt

Freshly ground black pepper
Butter for cooking the omelette

For the filling:
2½ tablespoons butter
1½ cups sliced small mushrooms
Freshly ground black pepper

Pinch finely chopped herbs
2 tablespoons natural yogurt *or*
  crème fraîche

Beat the eggs with the salt and pepper to taste in a bowl. Keep to one side. Make the filling by melting the butter in a small pan and gently sautéing the mushrooms until tender. Sprinkle with pepper while they are cooking. Stir in the herbs and yogurt and cook together for 2 minutes. Keep warm.

Put some melted butter in a hot omelette pan. Pour off the excess. Add the egg mixture and allow to solidify on the bottom of the pan. While the mixture is still liquid on the top, add the mushroom mixture. Cook the omelette until it solidifies a little more. Slide a spatula under the omelette and tip out onto a plate.

Mushrooms Provence-Style
(*Champignons à la Provençale*)

Serves 4

4 tablespoons olive oil
1 pound mushrooms, sliced
Salt
Freshly ground black pepper
2–4 cloves garlic, finely chopped
A few sage leaves
1 teaspoon chopped basil

1 teaspoon chopped oregano
3 tablespoons whole wheat
  breadcrumbs
Lemon juice
Black olives
1 tablespoon chopped parsley

Heat the oil in a heavy pan and gently sauté the mushrooms for 2 minutes. Season with salt and pepper to taste. Add the garlic and herbs and sauté together for 3 minutes. Add the breadcrumbs and sauté together for a further 3 minutes. Put on a serving dish and sprinkle with lemon juice. Garnish with olives and parsley.

Mushrooms with Cream Sauce
(*Champignons à la Crème*)

Serves 4

2 tablespoons olive oil
2 tablespoons melted butter
1 bunch scallions, sliced
¾ pound small mushrooms,
  sliced
1–2 cloves garlic, crushed

Salt
Freshly ground black pepper
½ cup heavy cream
½ cup natural yogurt *or* crème
  fraîche
1 tablespoon chopped parsley

Heat the oil and butter in a heavy pan and gently sauté the onions for 2 minutes. Add the mushrooms, garlic and salt and pepper to taste. Sauté together for 3 minutes. Stir in the cream and yogurt and allow to heat through. Do not allow the dish to boil. Serve garnished with the chopped parsley.

Stewed Mushrooms
(*Ragoût de Champignons*)

Serves 4

4 tablespoons olive oil
2 cloves garlic, finely chopped
1 tablespoon chopped parsley
1 pound small mushrooms, sliced
1 cup stock

½ cup dry red wine
Salt
Freshly ground black pepper
2 teaspoons chopped tarragon

Heat the oil in a heavy pan and sauté the garlic and parsley together for 2 minutes. Add the mushrooms and turn in the oil for 2 minutes. Add the stock, wine and salt and pepper to taste. Cover and stew together for 5 minutes. Serve garnished with the chopped herb.

Mushroom and Walnut Salad
(*Salade de Champignons aux Noix*)

Serves 4

This is an adaptation of a simple country recipe which uses truffles and walnuts, known as *Truffes et Cerneaux*. But both truffles and fresh walnuts are hard to come by. The truffle season opens in September and reaches its peak by mid-October. This coincides with the harvest of fresh walnuts.

¼ pound mushrooms *or* 4 black
  truffles
4 small lettuce hearts
Walnut *or* hazelnut oil

Wine vinegar
Salt
Freshly ground white pepper
16 fresh *or* mature walnuts

Finely slice the mushrooms or truffles and put in a serving bowl. Mix with the lettuce hearts and trickle a little oil and vinegar over. Sprinkle with salt and pepper. Scoop the fresh nuts from their shells or break mature nuts in halves. Stir into the mushroom and lettuce mixture. This salad is traditionally eaten with fresh bread and a light wine.

Mushroom Crêpes
(*Crêpes aux Champignons*)

Serves 6–8

For the crêpes:

1¼ cups whole wheat flour
Pinch salt
1½ cups liquid (½ milk,
    ½ water)

3 eggs
2 tablespoons melted butter *or*
    olive oil
Oil for cooking

For the filling:

4½ cups chopped mushrooms
¼ cup (½ stick) butter
Juice of ½ lemon

Salt
Freshly ground black pepper
Pinch freshly grated nutmeg

For the white sauce:

2¼ cups milk
1 tablespoon sliced onion
1 bay leaf
1 teaspoon peppercorns

Pinch freshly grated nutmeg
⅓ cup butter
½ cup whole wheat flour

6 tablespoons milk
6 tablespoons heavy cream *or*
    natural yogurt

¾ cup grated gruyère *or* cheddar
    cheese

First make the crêpes. Sift the flour and salt into a mixing bowl. Keep any bran in the sieve for adding to cereals or a bread mixture. Make a well in the center of the flour and add half the liquid. Gradually whisk together until a smooth batter is formed. Whisk in the eggs. Do not overbeat since this will make the crêpes tough. Stir in the melted butter and half the remaining liquid. Cover the bowl with a cloth and allow to stand for 1–2 hours. Just before the batter is needed, stir in enough of the remaining liquid to make a batter like thin cream.

Brush a 7-inch crêpe pan with oil and heat the pan gently until it begins to smoke. Spoon in enough batter to coat the bottom of the pan (2–3 tablespoons). Cook over moderate heat until both sides are golden. Turn out onto a plate and keep warm. Continue making crêpes in the same way until all the batter is used up.

Put the mushrooms, a third of the butter, the lemon juice, salt and pepper to taste and 2 tablespoons water into a saucepan. Cook together for a few minutes until the mushrooms are tender. Remove from the heat. Stir in the nutmeg.

Make the white sauce by bringing the milk just to a boil. Add the onion, bayleaf and peppercorns. Cover and allow to stand for 5 minutes. Melt the butter in a heavy pan and beat in the flour. Cook together over low heat, beating continually with a fork or whisk for 2 minutes. Allow to cool. Strain the seasoned milk and pour onto the flour mixture, beating continuously. Bring to a boil, then remove from the heat.

Stir half the sauce into the mushrooms. Spoon a tablespoon of mushroom mixture onto the center of each crêpe and roll up. Arrange in a greased ovenproof dish. Stir the milk and cream into the remaining sauce. Reheat and pour over the crêpes. Sprinkle with grated cheese. Melt the remaining butter and sprinkle over the cheese. Brown under the broiler and serve hot.

Mushrooms with Peppers
(*Champignons aux Poivrons*)   Serves 4

2 tablespoons olive oil
2 tablespoons melted butter
1 onion, finely chopped
1 green pepper, seeded and
   chopped, *or* 2 small green
   peppers
1 pound button mushrooms
1¼ cups finely chopped tomatoes

Salt
Freshly ground black pepper
1 teaspoon paprika
2 teaspoons chopped parsley
½ cup dry red wine
2 tablespoons natural yogurt *or*
   crème fraîche

Heat the oil and butter in a heavy pan and gently sauté the onion until just golden. Add the pepper, mushrooms and tomatoes and turn in the oil for 3 minutes. Season to taste and add the paprika and parsley. Stir together for 5 minutes. Add the wine and yogurt and cook together for 5 minutes.

Navy Beans

Soak and cook dried navy beans in the same way as described for chick peas.

Navy Bean Soup
(*Potage de Haricots*)

Serves 4

At the time of Pentecost (Pentecôte), a navy bean soup called "the soup of the Holy Ghost" is the traditional dish in the village of La Croix in the Alpes-Maritimes. It is made in two 33-gallon cauldrons in the local church.

3 tablespoons olive oil	1 teaspoon chopped basil
1 onion, finely chopped	1 teaspoon chopped sage
2 carrots, peeled and sliced	Salt
2 tomatoes, chopped	Freshly ground black pepper
2 cups cooked navy beans	6 cups vegetable stock *or* water
2 bay leaves	½ cup heavy cream *or* yogurt

Heat the oil in a heavy soup pot and sauté the onion until just golden. Add the carrots and tomatoes and turn in the hot oil for 5 minutes. Add the cooked beans, herbs and salt and pepper to taste. Stir together and add the stock. Cover and cook together over low heat for 15 minutes. Purée the soup in a blender or food processor and return to the pan. Stir in the cream and heat gently. Do not allow the soup to boil. Serve with sautéed or warm bread.

Navy Bean Salad
(*Salade de Haricots*)

Serves 4

3 cups cooked navy beans
1 small onion, finely sliced
2 stalks celery, sliced
Salt
Freshly ground black pepper

4 tablespoons olive oil
Juice of 1 lemon
1 tablespoon chopped parsley
2 tomatoes, cut in small pieces

Put the beans in a salad bowl and mix with the rest of the ingredients. Serve at room temperature or slightly chilled. Other herbs such as tarragon or sage could be substituted for the parsley.

Navy Bean Gratin
(*Gratin de Haricots Blancs*)

Serves 4

2 tablespoons olive oil
2 tablespoons melted butter
1 onion, finely chopped
2 cups cooked navy beans
Salt
Freshly ground black pepper
2¼ cups sliced mushrooms
6–8 black olives, pitted
   (optional)

1 teaspoon chopped sage
1 teaspoon chopped parsley
3 tablespoons whole wheat
   breadcrumbs
2 tablespoons crème fraîche *or*
   natural yogurt

Preheat the oven to 400°F. Heat the oil and butter in a heavy pan and sauté the onion until transparent. Add the beans and turn in the oil for 3 minutes. Season with salt and pepper to taste and add the mushrooms, olives and herbs. Cook together for 5 minutes. Put into a greased ovenproof dish and spread with the breadcrumbs. Spread the crème fraîche over and bake in the oven until the top is firm (15–20 minutes).

Navy Beans with Basil and Garlic
(*Haricots au Pistou*)

Serves 4

4 tablespoons olive oil
1 onion, sliced
1¼ cups chopped tomatoes
2–4 cloves garlic, sliced
3 cups parcooked navy beans

Salt
Freshly ground black pepper
1 teaspoon chopped thyme
1 teaspoon chopped marjoram
Vegetable stock

For the pistou:
4 cloves garlic
Handful fresh basil leaves

½ cup olive oil

Heat the oil in a heavy pan and gently sauté the onion until transparent. Add the tomatoes and garlic and turn in the oil for 5 minutes. Add the beans, salt and pepper to taste, thyme, marjoram and enough stock to cover the vegetables. Cover and cook over low heat until the beans are tender.

Meanwhile, make the pistou. Pound the garlic with the basil leaves to make a paste. Gradually add the olive oil, pounding to make a thick sauce. When the beans are cooked, stir into the pan and mix together well.

Navy Beans Poitou-Style
(*Haricots à la Poitevinne*)

Serves 4

The gastronomic area of Poitou is rich in agricultural produce and includes the départements of Vendée, Vienne, Deux-Sèvres and Maine-et-Loire.

1 onion, stuck with 2 cloves
1 large carrot, peeled and sliced
2 stalks celery, sliced
1 small parsnip *or* piece of
  rutabaga, sliced
2 cloves garlic, sliced
Salt
Freshly ground black pepper

1 teaspoon chopped thyme
1 teaspoon chopped marjoram
3 cups cooked navy beans
½ cup heavy cream *or* natural
  yogurt
2 teaspoons chopped parsley
2 teaspoons chopped basil

Put the onion, carrot, celery, parsnip and garlic in a pan and sprinkle with salt and pepper to taste. Cover with water and stir in the thyme and marjoram. Cover and allow to cook together over low heat until all the vegetables are tender. Drain. The cooking liquid may be used as stock. Put all the vegetables back in the pan. Remove the cloves from the onion and slice. Add the beans and cream. Turn together over low heat, adding a little of the cooking liquid if needed to make a sauce. Serve garnished with the chopped parsley and basil.

Southern Bean Stew
(*Cassoulet aux Légumes*)

Serves 4

The term *cassoulet* comes from *cassoule*, a glazed earthenware casserole, reddish in color, made near Castelnaudary in the ancient region of Languedoc. This cassoulet is an adaptation of the traditional dish. You can vary the ingredients to suit your taste, but typically it should include navy beans.

2 tablespoons olive oil
1 tablespoon melted butter
1 onion, chopped
1¼ cups chopped carrots
2–4 cloves garlic, finely chopped
Handful mixed herbs
¾ cup cooked navy beans
¾ cup cooked chick peas
¾ cup string beans, snapped in pieces

2–4 tomatoes, chopped
½ cup frozen *or* parcooked fresh peas
1¼ cups chopped zucchini
1 cup vegetable stock
Salt
Freshly ground black pepper
1 cup whole wheat breadcrumbs

Preheat the oven to 400°F. Heat the oil and butter in a casserole dish and gently sauté the onion until transparent. Add the carrots, garlic, herbs, beans and chick peas and cook together for 5 minutes. Add the tomatoes, peas, zucchini and stock. Season with salt and pepper to taste and cook together for 20 minutes. Cover with the breadcrumbs and bake in the oven until the top is crisp and golden (about 15 minutes).

Onions

Onion Soup
(*Soupe à l'Oignon*)

Serves 4

3 pounds onions
⅓ cup butter
1 teaspoon soft brown sugar
5 cups vegetable stock
Salt

Freshly ground black pepper
4 thick slices French bread
1 cup grated gruyère *or* cheddar
  cheese

Put one onion to one side and slice the rest. Put half the butter in a soup pot and sauté the sliced onions over low heat until they begin to turn golden. Do not allow them to burn. Peel the whole onion and cut a slice off the top and bottom. Dip the sliced ends in sugar. Melt a tablespoon of butter in a small saucepan and cook the whole onion over low heat until the sugar caramelizes. Pour the onion and any melted butter into the soup pot. Add the stock and salt and pepper to taste. Bring to a boil and simmer for 10 minutes. Discard the whole onion.

Just before serving, lightly toast the bread slices and put into four ovenproof bowls. Pour in the soup and sprinkle with a good layer of cheese. Melt the remaining butter and trickle over each bowl. Put the bowls under the broiler and brown the cheese. Serve hot.

Onion Fritters
(Beignets d'Oignons)   Serves 4

½ cup whole wheat flour
Pinch salt
2 teaspoons olive oil
1 egg white
1 pound onions

Freshly ground black pepper
Oil for deep-frying
Lemon slices
2 teaspoons chopped parsley

To make the batter, sift the flour and salt together in a bowl. Make a well in the center and pour in the oil and 3 tablespoons of lukewarm water. Gradually mix with the flour until a smooth creamy batter is formed, adding another 2 or 3 tablespoons of water if needed. Leave to one side for 30 minutes. Just before the batter is needed, beat the egg white well and fold into the batter. Mix well.

Meanwhile, peel and trim the onions and slice. Put on a plate and sprinkle with salt and pepper. When the batter is ready, heat the oil in a heavy pan. Bring the batter near the heat. When the oil is hot, put all the onion slices into the batter. Mix well and then fry the slices in hot oil until golden. Allow to drain on paper towels and arrange on a serving dish with slices of lemon. Garnish with the chopped parsley.

Onion Omelette
(Omelette aux Oignons)   Makes 1

At harvest time *(moissons)* in the Midi, part of the work contract was five meals a day. At 1 P.M. the harvest worker would be given a bowl of soup and a thick onion omelette with some bread.

3 tablespoons melted butter
1 onion, sliced
Salt

Freshly ground black pepper
2 teaspoons chopped herbs
2 eggs, beaten

Heat the butter in an omelette pan and gently sauté the onions until just golden. Season with salt and pepper to taste. In a separate bowl, beat the herbs with the eggs. Pour in the sautéed onions, leaving a coating of butter in the frying pan. Turn up the heat a little and add the onion and egg mixture. Allow it to spread over the bottom of the pan. Slip out onto a plate just before the omelette is completely set.

Onion Gratin
(Gratin d'Oignons)   Serves 4

2 tablespoons olive oil
2 tablespoons melted butter
2 cups chopped onions
2–4 cloves garlic, finely chopped
2¼ cups sliced mushrooms
Salt
Freshly ground black pepper

1 tablespoon chopped parsley
1 teaspoon chopped oregano
½ cup crème fraîche *or* natural
   yogurt
3 tablespoons whole wheat
   breadcrumbs
Freshly grated nutmeg

Peheat the oven to 375°F. Heat the oil and butter in a heavy pan and sauté the onions over low heat for 5 minutes. Add the garlic and sauté for 2 minutes. Add the mushrooms and season with salt and pepper to taste. Turn in the oil for 3 minutes. Add the herbs and crème fraîche and cook together for 5 minutes. Turn into a well-greased ovenproof dish and cover with the breadcrumbs. Sprinkle with nutmeg and bake in the oven until the top is golden (about 30 minutes).

Onion Quiche
(Quiche aux Oignons)   Serves 4

For the pastry:
1 cup whole wheat self-rising
   flour *or* 1 cup whole wheat
   flour and 1 teaspoon baking
   powder
Pinch salt
2½ tablespoons butter, chilled
   and cut in pieces

2½ tablespoons margarine,
   chilled and cut in pieces
1 teaspoon soft brown sugar
3 tablespoons cold water
1 tablespoon olive oil

For the filling:
3 tablespoons olive oil
1 tablespoon melted butter
4 small onions, thinly sliced
Salt

Freshly ground black pepper
2 eggs
3 tablespoons heavy cream *or*
   natural yogurt

First make the quiche pastry. Sift the flour with the salt in a mixing bowl. Add the chilled butter and margarine with a knife and cut into the flour. Make into crumbs with the fingertips. In a separate bowl dissolve the sugar in the water and stir in the oil. Gradually add this mixture to the flour until a soft, pliable dough is formed which comes away from the sides of the bowl. You may not need all of the liquid. Use flour to make into a ball. Wrap in plastic wrap and put in the refrigerator or a cool place for 20 minutes. After 10 minutes preheat the oven to 400°F.

Meanwhile, make the filling. Heat the oil and butter in a heavy pan and gently sauté the onion until transparent. Season with salt and pepper to taste. Sauté together until the onions are golden. Remove from the heat. Beat the eggs and cream together in a bowl.

Roll out the pastry on a floured board and place in a greased 8–9-inch pie plate or tart pan with a removable base. Pull the pastry up the sides of the pan. Prick all over with a fork. Bake in the oven until the pastry has set (5–7 minutes). Allow to cool for a few minutes.

Arrange the onions in the quiche base and spread over. Spoon in the egg mixture to fill in any gaps and to just cover the onions. Bake in the oven for 30 minutes. Allow to cool for a few minutes before removing from the pan. Serve hot or cold.

Stewed Onions
(*Ragoût d'Oignons*)

Serves 4

3 tablespoons olive oil
1 tablespoon melted butter
1 pound small onions, thickly sliced
1–2 cloves garlic, sliced
Salt
Freshly ground black pepper

1¼ cups chopped tomatoes
1 teaspoon chopped thyme
1 teaspoon chopped basil
1 tablespoon chopped parsley
½ cup vegetable stock
1 cup dry wine

Heat the oil and butter in a heavy pan and gently sauté the onions until transparent. Add the garlic and season with salt and pepper to taste. Add the tomatoes and herbs and turn in the oil for 3 minutes. Add the stock and wine. Cover and allow to stew for 20 minutes.

Onions in Sweet and Sour Sauce
(*Confiture d'Oignons*)

Serves 4

This is typical of a new generation of tastes and textures pioneered by such celebrated chefs as Michel Guérard. Once you have appreciated the blend of vegetable, fruit and sugar, you are ready to begin your own experiments in combination. Like all the new dishes, delicate presentation is important.

½ cup (1 stick) butter
1½ pounds small onions, thinly
  sliced
1 cup confectioner's sugar
1 teaspoon salt
½ teaspoon freshly ground black
  pepper

3 tablespoons sherry
3 tablespoons wine vinegar
2–3 dried apricots
1 cup red wine

Gently heat the butter in a saucepan until it just begins to brown. Add the onions, sugar, and salt and pepper. Cover and allow to simmer for 30 minutes, stirring from time to time. Add the sherry, vinegar, apricots and wine. Leave the lid off and cook for a further 30 minutes over low heat.

Parsnips

Parsnip Croquettes
(*Croquettes de Panais*)

1 pound parsnips
Salt
2 tablespoons melted butter
Freshly ground black pepper
Pinch freshly grated nutmeg
Whole wheat flour

1 egg, beaten
Whole wheat breadcrumbs
Oil for frying
Lemon wedges
Sprig of parsley

Peel and trim the parsnips and slice. Boil in slightly salted water until tender. Drain and mash. Season with salt, pepper and nutmeg. Add a little flour to make a lump which can easily be divided into 12 balls. Roll each ball in flour and flatten a little with the hands. Leave to one side for 20 minutes. Dip each croquette first in beaten egg, then roll in breadcrumbs. Fry in hot oil until golden on both sides. Put on a serving dish with lemon wedges. Garnish with parsley.

This recipe could be used with other root vegetables such as carrots, rutabagas or turnips.

Parsnip Loaf
(*Pain au Panais*)

Serves 4–6

1½ pounds parsnips
Salt
2 tablespoons olive oil
1 small onion, sliced
½ cup whole wheat flour

Freshly ground black pepper
3 eggs
2 tablespoons milk *or* cream *or* yogurt
Butter

Peel and trim the parsnips and slice. Boil in slightly salted water until tender. Preheat the oven to 400°F. Drain the parsnips and mash. Heat the olive oil in a frying pan and sauté the onion until just golden. Mix in the mashed parsnip and heat through. Remove from the heat. In a mixing bowl, combine the flour with a little salt and pepper, the eggs, milk and a tablespoon of melted butter. Gradually beat together and let stand for 30 minutes. Mix in the parsnip mixture. Put into a well-buttered ovenproof dish and bake in the oven until the loaf is firm (30–40 minutes).

The loaf may be served with a sauce of your choice.

Peas

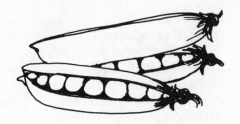

Peasant's Peas
(*Petits Pois à la Paysanne*)

Serves 4

Typical of the country style, use whatever odds and ends of vegetables you have at hand.

2 tablespoons olive oil
2 tablespoons melted butter
1 onion, sliced
2 carrots, trimmed and sliced
2 potatoes, cut in small chunks
2–4 cloves garlic, finely chopped
2¼ cups shelled peas
Salt

Freshly ground black pepper
1 teaspoon chopped sage
1 teaspoon chopped basil
2 teaspoons chopped parsley
2 tablespoons natural yogurt *or* crème fraîche
½ cup dry wine
½ cup vegetable stock

Heat the oil and butter in a heavy pan and gently sauté the onion until just golden. Add the carrots, potatoes, garlic and peas and turn in the oil for 3 minutes. Season with salt and pepper to taste and add the herbs. Cook together for 5 minutes. Add the yogurt, wine and stock. Cover and cook together until all the vegetables are tender.

Pea Soup
(Potage St. Germain) Serves 4

3¾ cups vegetable stock
3 sprigs fresh mint
1⅔ cups fresh *or* frozen peas
Salt
Freshly ground black pepper

½ cup cream *or* natural yogurt
1 teaspoon soft brown sugar
2½ tablespoons butter, cut into
  small pieces

Put the stock, 2 mint sprigs, peas and salt and pepper to taste in a heavy soup pot and simmer together until the peas are tender. Discard the mint sprigs. Purée the soup in a blender or food processor. Stir in half the cream and the sugar and gently heat the soup. Do not allow to boil. Stir in the butter. Meanwhile, finely chop the third mint sprig.

Pour the soup into separate bowls. Add a spoonful of cream to each helping and garnish with a little chopped mint.

Peas with Lettuce and Cream Sauce
(Petits Pois à la Française) Serves 6

¼ cup (½ stick) butter
6 cups parcooked fresh peas *or*
  frozen peas
1 lettuce, trimmed and
  quartered
1 bunch scallions, trimmed and
  thickly sliced
1 teaspoon chopped mint

1 teaspoon chopped parsley
Salt
Freshly ground black pepper
1 teaspoon soft brown sugar
2 tablespoons cream
2 tablespoons natural yogurt *or*
  crème fraîche

Heat the butter in a heavy pan and add the peas, lettuce, scallions and herbs. Turn in the hot butter for 3 minutes. Season with salt and pepper to taste. Add the sugar. Cover and simmer for 10 minutes. Stir in the cream and yogurt and allow to heat through. Do not allow the dish to boil.

Fava beans may also be prepared this way.

Peas with Onions

(*Petits Pois aux Oignons*)

Serves 4–6

2 pounds fresh peas
Salt
2 tablespoons olive oil
2 tablespoons melted butter
1 onion, sliced

2 tablespoons whole wheat flour
1 tablespoon lemon juice
1 teaspoon soft brown sugar
Freshly ground black pepper
1 tablespoon chopped parsley

Cook the peas in boiling, slightly salted water until tender. Drain but reserve the cooking liquid. Heat the oil and butter in a heavy pan and gently sauté the onion until transparent. Raise the heat and allow to turn just golden. Lower the heat and gradually stir in the flour. Remove from the heat and gradually stir in 2 cups of pea water or an equivalent amount of vegetable stock, stirring all the time. Heat again for 2 minutes. Add the lemon juice, sugar and peas. Season with salt and pepper to taste and cook together for 5 minutes. Serve sprinkled with chopped parsley.

Peppers

Pepper and Tomato Omelette
(*Omelette aux Poivron et Tomates*)

Serves 4–6

4 tablespoons olive oil
1 small onion, finely chopped
1 green pepper, seeded and
  chopped
1¼ cups chopped tomatoes
2–3 cloves garlic, finely chopped

2 teaspoons chopped basil
2 teaspoons chopped parsley
Salt
Freshly ground black pepper
6 eggs
Butter

Heat the oil in a heavy pan and sauté the onion until just golden. Add the pepper, tomatoes, garlic and herbs and turn in the oil for 5 minutes. Season with salt and pepper to taste. Beat the eggs together until well mixed. Put a heavy frying pan over low heat and heat some butter. When the butter is melted, pour off the excess. Pour in the egg mixture. When the bottom of the omelette begins to solidify, add the pepper and tomato mixture. Continue cooking until the omelette is almost set. Turn out onto a plate and cut into portions.

Peppers and Scrambled Egg
(*Piperade*)

Serves 2

This is one of the many versions of the classic Basque dish.

3 tablespoons olive oil
1 small onion, sliced
2 tomatoes, chopped
1 clove garlic, finely chopped
Salt

Freshly ground black pepper
1 red *or* green pepper, seeded
  and cut into small pieces
6 eggs, beaten

Heat the oil in a heavy pan. Add the onion and gently sauté until transparent and soft. Add the tomatoes, garlic and salt and pepper to taste and cook over low heat for 10 minutes. Stir in the pepper and cook for a further 5 minutes. Beat the eggs until frothy and stir them into the tomato mixture. Cook together over low heat until the eggs are cooked but still moist. Serve hot.

Pepper and Rice Salad
(*Salade de Riz aux Poivrons*)   Serves 4

4 cups cooked rice
½ green pepper, seeded and
    chopped
½ red pepper, seeded and
    chopped
1 tablespoon chopped chives
1 tablespoon chopped parsley *or*
    basil

2 teaspoons chopped oregano
Salt
Freshly ground black pepper
1 tablespoon chopped tarragon
Olive oil
Wine vinegar

Put the rice into a salad bowl and mix in the peppers, chives, parsley and oregano. Season with salt and pepper to taste. Sprinkle with chopped tarragon. Serve with olive oil and vinegar so that a vinaigrette can be made to taste.

Baked Peppers
(*Poivrons au Four*)   Serves 4

1 green pepper
1 red pepper
1 onion
2¼ cups sliced mushrooms
1-2 cloves garlic, crushed
Sprig of thyme
Sprig of parsley

Salt
Freshly ground black pepper
3 tablespoons olive oil
1 tablespoon melted butter
3 tablespoons crème fraîche *or*
    natural yogurt

Preheat the oven to 375°F. Seed the peppers and cut into slices. Trim the onion and slice. Put the sliced vegetables (including mushrooms) in a well-greased ovenproof dish. Add the garlic and herbs. Sprinkle salt and pepper over to taste. Drizzle the oil and melted butter over and spread with crème fraîche. Bake in the oven until the peppers are tender (35–45 minutes).

Potatoes

The "earth-apple" was introduced into France as an ornamental plant around 1540. In 1630, cultivation of the potato was still banned for fear of leprosy and it was considered unfit for human consumption until 1771. However, in 1773 Parmentier published his *Chemical Examination of Potato, Wheat and Rice* and from then on the potato gradually became more and more popular. It is now an important part of the French diet.

Potato and Bean Salad
(Salade de Pommes de Terre et Haricots)   Serves 4

1⅔ cups diced potatoes
1⅔ cups navy beans
Salt
1 tablespoon lemon juice
Freshly ground black pepper
1 teaspoon Dijon mustard
6 tablespoons olive oil

1 clove garlic, crushed
1 small cucumber, sliced
10 black olives, pitted and halved
3 medium tomatoes, cut in quarters

Boil the potatoes and beans in separate pans in slightly salted water until tender. Meanwhile make up the dressing. Whisk the lemon juice with a good pinch of salt and pepper and the mustard. Gradually whisk in the oil and garlic until the sauce is well blended. Put the cooked vegetables in a large salad bowl with the cucumber and mix together with the dressing. Arrange the olives over the top of the salad and the tomatoes around the edge of the bowl.

Potato and Cream Pie
(*Pâté Bourbonnais*)

Serves 4–6

For the pastry:
1 cup whole wheat flour
1 cup self-rising flour
Pinch salt

¼ cup (½ stick) margarine
¼ cup (½ stick) butter
Cold water

For the filling:
1½ pounds parcooked potatoes
1 small onion, chopped
2 tablespoons chopped parsley
2 cloves garlic, finely chopped
Salt

Freshly ground black pepper
2½ tablespoons butter
½–1 cup heavy cream *or* crème
   fraîche

Make the pastry by sifting the flour and salt into a mixing bowl. Cut the butter and margarine into pieces and rub into the flour with the fingertips to make crumbs. Sprinkle 2 tablespoons of water over and squeeze into the flour. Gradually add a little water at a time until a smooth dough is formed. Make up into a ball and wrap in plastic wrap. Put in the refrigerator for 30 minutes to rest.

Preheat the oven to 400°F. In a bowl mix together the potatoes, onion, parsley and garlic with salt and pepper to taste. Grease a 9½-inch metal pie dish. Roll out two-thirds of the pastry on a floured board and line the pie dish. Put in the potato filling. Melt the butter and trickle over the mixture. Roll out the rest of the pastry to make a top crust for the pie. Moisten the edge of the pastry lining and press on the lid. Press around the edge with a fork. Prick a few holes in the top crust and bake in the oven until the crust is golden (about 30 minutes). Remove from the oven. Make a small hole in the center of the pie lid. Carefully pour in the cream. Serve hot or cold.

Potato Gratin
(*Gratin Dauphinois*)   Serves 4

This is one of the classic dishes of France. It excels in simplicity of preparation and taste. Although many versions abound in France, the original is a nourishing mountain dish from the Alps of the Dauphiné.

2 pounds potatoes
1–2 cloves garlic, finely chopped
Salt
Freshly ground black pepper

2 cups heavy cream
2½ tablespoons butter, cut in pieces

Preheat the oven to 300°F. Peel the potatoes and slice as thinly as possible (old books mention "gold pieces"). Layer into an earthenware gratin dish, sprinkling with garlic, salt and pepper as you put the potato slices in. Pour the cream over. Dot with pieces of butter. Cover loosely with foil. Put in the oven to bake for 1½ hours. Remove the foil and turn up the oven to 350°F to brown the top (about 10 minutes).

Potato and Cheese Cake
(*Galette de Pommes de Terre*)   Serves 4

1 pound potatoes
Salt
2 tablespoons melted butter
1 cup grated gruyère *or* cheddar cheese

Freshly ground black pepper
Freshly grated nutmeg
Olive oil for sautéing
1 tablespoon chopped parsley
Lemon wedges

Boil the potatoes in slightly salted water until soft. Drain and peel. In a bowl mash with the butter, cheese, pepper, nutmeg and a pinch of salt. Heat a few tablespoons of oil in a heavy frying pan and put in the potato mixture. Pat down with a slice to make a cake-like shape and allow to brown on the bottom. Put a plate on the top and tip out onto the plate. Put the potato cake back in the pan the other way up to brown the other side. Add a little more oil if necessary. Serve garnished with parsley and lemon wedges.

Potatoes with Herbs
(*Pommes de Terre à la Paysanne*)
Serves 4

This dish reflects the country style of adding wild plants to a simple dish, bringing color and extra nourishment at no extra cost.

1½ pounds potatoes
Salt
2 tablespoons melted butter
2 tablespoons olive oil
1 onion, sliced
2 tablespoons whole wheat flour
1½ cups vegetable stock

½ cup dry wine
1-2 cloves garlic, finely chopped
A good handful fresh herbs such
  as chervil, sorrel, dandelion,
  borage, parsley
Freshly ground black pepper

Preheat the oven to 350°F. Boil the potatoes in slightly salted water for 10 minutes. Drain and slice. Put in the bottom of a greased ovenproof dish. In a separate pan, heat the butter and oil and gently sauté the onion until just golden. Stir in the flour and sauté for 2 minutes. Gradually add the stock and wine. Stir together and pour over the potato slices. Put in the garlic. Scatter over the herbs and season with salt and pepper to taste. Mix together. Cover and bake in the oven for 1 hour. After 30 minutes remove the lid.

Potato Soup
(*Potage des Vendanges*)
Serves 4

Les vendanges is the grape harvest. This nourishing soup is typical of those served to grape pickers during this season of hard work.

3 tablespoons melted butter
2 leeks, trimmed, washed and
  chopped
1 pound potatoes, cut in pieces
6 cups vegetable stock
1 bay leaf

1 tablespoon chopped parsley
Salt
Freshly ground black pepper
1 cup cottage cheese *or* crème
  fraîche
1 tablespoon chopped tarragon

Heat the butter in a heavy pan and cook the leeks until they soften. Add the potatoes and turn in the butter for 3 minutes. Add the stock, herbs and salt and pepper to taste. Cook over low heat until the potatoes are tender. Purée in a blender or food processor. Return to the pan and stir in the cottage cheese. Serve garnished with chopped tarragon.

Potato Omelette
(*Omelette Paysanne*)

Serves 2

2 tablespoons olive oil
1 small onion, finely chopped
½ cup chopped tomatoes
1 medium potato, cooked and diced
2 tablespoons finely chopped parsley *or* other fresh herb

4 eggs
Salt
Freshly ground black pepper
2½ tablespoons butter

Heat the oil in a heavy frying pan and sauté the onion until transparent. Add the tomatoes and potato and cook together until the potato begins to turn golden. Add the herbs and remove from the heat. Beat the eggs in a bowl with salt and pepper to taste. Heat the butter in an omelette pan and pour in the egg mixture. Stir well for 10 seconds with the flat of a fork until the eggs begin to solidify. Tip the pan so that any uncooked egg mixture can flow to the sides. Continue cooking until the eggs are almost set. Stir in the sautéed vegetables and stir for a few seconds. Cook for a further few seconds to brown the bottom of the omelette. The top should be almost firm. Remove from the heat. Put a plate over the top of the pan and tip out the omelette. Slide the omelette back into the pan to brown the other side. Tip out onto a serving plate and cut into wedges. Serve hot or cold.

Potatoes Midi-Style
(*Tian du Midi*)

Serves 4–6

Tian is a Provençal word for a thick cake-like dish. It may be fried in a pan or finished in the oven.

2 pounds potatoes	1 teaspoon chopped basil
Oil for frying	1 teaspoon chopped oregano
⅔ cup sliced onions	1 teaspoon chopped parsley
1 cup grated parmesan *or* cheddar cheese	Salt
	Freshly ground black pepper
1 teaspoon chopped thyme	1 pound tomatoes, sliced

Parcook the potatoes in boiling water. Drain and peel. Allow to cool and slice. Preheat the oven to 375°F. Heat a few tablespoons of oil in a heavy pan and fry the potato slices until just golden. Drain on paper towels. Put a layer of potato slices in the bottom of a greased ovenproof dish. Cover with a layer of onions. Sprinkle with cheese. Mix the herbs together and sprinkle some over the cheese. Add a pinch of salt and pepper. Cover with a layer of tomato slices. Put in a similar layer of potatoes, onions, cheese, herbs and tomatoes. When all the ingredients are used up, bake in the oven for 30 minutes.

Pumpkins

Pumpkin Soufflé
(*Soufflé de Potiron*)

Serves 4–6

1 pound pumpkin
Salt
½ tablespoon whole wheat flour
2 cups milk
Freshly ground black pepper

3 eggs
3 heaping tablespoons grated
  gruyère *or* cheddar cheese
1 teaspoon chopped herbs

Preheat the oven to 375°F. Peel and seed the pumpkin and cut into small pieces. Put in a pan and just cover with water. Sprinkle on a pinch of salt and boil the pumpkin until soft. Drain well and mash. Press out any excess moisture. Put the flour in a cup and add a little milk. Stir together until there are no lumps. Heat the rest of the milk in a pan and pour in the flour mixture. Season with salt and pepper and heat gently until the milk thickens, stirring all the time. Allow to cool and whisk in the mashed pumpkin. Separate the egg yolks from the whites and whisk the yolks into the pumpkin mixture. Stir in the cheese and herbs. When the mixture is cold, beat the egg whites until stiff and fold into the pumpkin mixture. Pour the mixture into a well-buttered soufflé or ovenproof dish and bake in the oven until the mixture has risen and turned golden (about 30 minutes). Serve immediately.

Pumpkin Pancakes
(*Galettes de Potiron*)

Makes 16–20

1 cup chopped pumpkin
Milk
2 eggs, beaten
2 teaspoons olive oil

Pinch salt
1½ cups whole wheat flour
Oil for cooking
Lemon wedges

Peel and seed the pumpkin and cut into small chunks. Boil in water until soft. Purée in a blender or food processor. Add enough milk to make up to 2¼ cups of liquid. Beat in the eggs, oil and salt until well blended. Gradually stir in the flour until a smooth batter is obtained. Allow the batter to stand for 30 minutes before use. Heat a little oil in a heavy frying pan. Pour off the excess. Pour in enough batter to cover the bottom of the pan. Allow it to cook for 2–3 minutes then turn over and cook on the other side. Turn out onto a plate. Keep warm and serve with lemon wedges.

Butter may also be used for the cooking. Take care not to let it burn.

Pumpkin Gratin
(*Gratin de Potiron*)

Serves 4

2 pounds pumpkin
6 cloves garlic, finely chopped
4 tablespoons chopped parsley
1 teaspoon chopped thyme
1 teaspoon chopped mint
Salt
Freshly ground black pepper

4 tablespoons whole wheat flour
2 tablespoons natural yogurt *or*
  crème fraîche
4 tablespoons olive oil
3 tablespoons whole wheat
  breadcrumbs

Preheat the oven to 350°F. Peel the pumpkin and seed. Cut into very small pieces. On a plate, mix together the garlic, herbs, salt and pepper to taste and flour. Roll the pumpkin pieces in this mixture and put them in a well-greased ovenproof dish. Spread the yogurt over and trickle over 3 tablespoons of oil. Cover with the breadcrumbs and trickle over the rest of the oil. Bake in the oven for about 1 hour until the top is golden and the pumpkin pieces are tender.

Pumpkin Soup
(*Soupe au Potiron*)

Serves 4

¼ cup (½ stick) butter
½ onion, finely chopped
1-pound piece pumpkin
2 cloves garlic, finely chopped
Salt
Freshly ground black pepper

2 teaspoons chopped basil
2 teaspoons chopped parsley
6 cups stock
4 tablespoons whole wheat
   breadcrumbs
1 tablespoon olive oil

Heat the butter in a heavy soup pot and gently sauté the onion until transparent. Peel the pumpkin and cut in small pieces. Add to the onion with the garlic. Season with salt and pepper to taste. Turn in the hot butter for 4 minutes. Add the herbs and stock. Cover and simmer until the pumpkin is tender. Purée the soup in a blender or food processor. Sauté the breadcrumbs in oil until golden. Stir into the soup. Serve hot.

Salsify

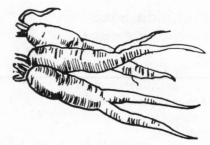

Vegetable Terrine with Salsify
(*Terrine de Légumes aux Salsifis*)   Serves 4

Here is a way of serving this unusual root vegetable with an easily prepared terrine.

4 tablespoons olive oil
3 cups diced eggplant
3 cups chopped mushrooms
⅔ cup peeled and chopped
  carrots
2½ cups fresh spinach
2 eggs

Salt
Freshly ground black pepper
Freshly grated nutmeg
1½ pounds fresh salsify
Lemon juice
1 tablespoon flour

Preheat the oven to 350°F. Line a 4½ × 8½-inch bread loaf pan with waxed paper. Heat the oil in a heavy pan and gently sauté the eggplant, mushrooms and carrots until the vegetables are tender (about 10 minutes). Meanwhile tear the spinach leaves in pieces and steam them for 10 minutes. Press out as much juice as possible and chop. Put all the sautéed vegetables in a bowl and mash together or put in a food processor and blend. Add the eggs and seasoning to taste and blend again.

Put one third of this mixture in the bottom of the loaf pan. Add the spinach and spread out evenly. Put in the rest of the sautéed vegetable mixture and smooth out. Lightly rest a piece of waxed paper on the top and bake in the oven until the terrine is firm and just beginning to shrink away from the sides of the pan (35–40 minutes). Remove from the oven and allow to cool, then refrigerate for at least 2 hours.

Meanwhile, prepare the salsify. Wash and peel with a potato peeler, holding the roots flat on the table. Cut them into short (2 inch) lengths and put in a bowl of water. Add a few drops of lemon juice to prevent the salsify from discoloring. Fill a saucepan with 4 cups of water into which a tablespoon of flour has been whisked. Season with a little lemon juice and salt. Bring to a gentle boil. Drain the salsify and add to the flour liquid *(blanc)*. Allow to simmer for 45 minutes. Allow to cool in the blanc. Drain when needed.

Serve slices of cooled terrine with salsify or a sauce if salsify is unavailable.

Spinach

Baked Spinach
(*Épinards au Four*)

Serves 4

1½ pounds spinach
2 tablespoons olive oil
1 tablespoon melted butter
1 small onion, finely chopped
¾ cup chopped tomatoes
1-2 cloves garlic, finely chopped
Salt
Freshly ground black pepper

1 tablespoon chopped parsley
1 teaspoon chopped thyme
1 teaspoon chopped sage
2 tablespoons whole wheat flour
3 eggs, beaten
1 egg yolk
⅔ cup milk

Preheat the oven to 400°F. Wash the spinach and blanch in boiling water for 3 minutes. Drain thoroughly and chop. Heat the oil and butter in a heavy pan and gently sauté the onion until transparent. Add the tomatoes, garlic, salt and pepper to taste and turn in the oil for 3 minutes. Add the spinach and herbs and mix well over low heat for a few minutes. Remove from the heat. In a separate bowl, beat the flour into the eggs and egg yolk. Stir in the milk. Pour into the spinach mixture. Put the mixture in a greased ovenproof dish and bake in the oven until the eggs are set and the top is a little golden in color (30–40 minutes). Allow to cool for a few minutes before serving.

Spinach Soufflé
(Soufflé aux Épinards)   Serves 4

2 cups spinach	2 tablespoons whole wheat flour
Salt	1⅛ cups boiling milk
Butter	Freshly ground black pepper
4 tablespoons grated parmesan,	Pinch freshly grated nutmeg
gruyère *or* cheddar cheese	4 egg yolks
1 tablespoon chopped scallion	5 egg whites

Preheat the oven to 400°F. Blanch the spinach in slightly salted, boiling water for 4 minutes. Drain well and chop. Butter a soufflé dish (6 cup) and sprinkle with 1 tablespoon of the grated cheese. Heat a tablespoon of butter in a pan and gently sauté the scallion for 1 minute. Add the spinach and a pinch of salt and cook until most of the spinach moisture has evaporated. Remove from the heat.

Prepare the soufflé sauce base by melting ¼ cup (½ stick) butter in a heavy saucepan. Stir in the flour with a wooden spoon and stir with the butter for 2 minutes. Remove from the heat. When the mixture has stopped foaming, pour in the boiling milk. Beat well with a whisk until blended. Whisk in a pinch of salt, pepper and nutmeg. Put back over moderate heat and stir together until the sauce thickens (about 1–2 minutes). Stir in the egg yolks and remove from the heat. Stir in the spinach mixture.

Beat the egg whites with a whisk until stiff. Stir a quarter of the egg whites into the sauce base. Stir in 2 tablespoons of the grated cheese. Fold in the rest of the egg whites and turn the mixture into the soufflé dish. Sprinkle with the last tablespoon of cheese and put in the oven. Turn down the heat to 375°F and bake until the soufflé has turned golden and risen well (25–30 minutes).

Spinach Patties
(Petits Pâtés d'Épinards)

Makes 6

1½ pounds spinach
4 cloves garlic, finely chopped
½ teaspoon salt
Freshly ground black pepper

Freshly grated nutmeg
Whole wheat flour
Oil for deep-frying
Lemon slices

Wash the spinach, remove any coarse stalks and chop. Blanch in 2 cups
of boiling water for 3 minutes. Drain thoroughly. Purée in a blender or
food processor. Put into a bowl and add the garlic, salt, pepper, nutmeg
and enough flour to make a firm mixture. Roll into 6 large balls, flatten
slightly with the fingers and make into patties with the aid of a little
flour. Fry in oil until golden on both sides. Drain on paper towels. Serve
with lemon slices.

Spinach Gratin
(Gratin d'Épinards)

Serves 4

1½ pounds spinach
2 tablespoons melted butter
1 small onion, sliced
Salt
Freshly grated nutmeg
Freshly ground black pepper

3 tablespoons crème fraîche or
  natural yogurt
2 tablespoons whole wheat
  breadcrumbs
2 tablespoons grated parmesan,
  gruyère or cheddar cheese

Preheat the oven to 400°F. Blanch the spinach in boiling water for 3
minutes. Drain thoroughly and chop. Heat the butter in a heavy pan
and sauté the onion until just golden. Add the spinach and seasonings
and turn in the hot butter for 3 minutes. Put in a greased ovenproof dish
and spread with the crème fraîche. Mix the breadcrumbs with the
grated cheese and spread over the crème fraîche. Bake in the oven until
the top is crisp and golden (about 30 minutes).

Spinach with Poached Eggs

(Oeufs Pochés Florentine)   Serves 4 *or* 8 as an appetizer

Recipes with the word *florentine* traditionally contain spinach, which was thought to have been introduced into French cuisine from Florence by Catherine de Medici.

2½ pounds fresh spinach
8 eggs
2½ tablespoons butter
Salt
Freshly ground black pepper
Freshly grated nutmeg

2 egg yolks
¾ cup grated gruyère *or* cheddar
  cheese
1 teaspoon Dijon mustard
4 tablespoons milk

For the white sauce:
2 cups milk
2 slices onion
1 bay leaf

6 peppercorns
2½ tablespoons butter
2 tablespoons whole wheat flour

Blanch the spinach in boiling water for 4 minutes, drain thoroughly and chop. Keep warm.

Make the white sauce by bringing the milk to a boil. Remove from the heat. Add the onion, bay leaf and peppercorns. Cover and allow to stand for 5 minutes. Heat the butter in a heavy saucepan and whisk in the flour. Whisk together over low heat for 2 minutes. Strain the aromatized milk onto this mixture, whisking continuously. Bring the sauce to a boil and remove from the heat. Meanwhile, poach the eggs.

Melt 2½ tablespoons butter and stir into the warm spinach. Stir in salt, pepper and nutmeg to taste. Spread over the bottom of a greased ovenproof dish. Turn on the broiler to preheat. Drain the poached eggs and arrange on the spinach. Beat the egg yolks, two-thirds of the cheese and the mustard into the white sauce. The sauce should thickly coat the spoon. If it is too thick, stir in a little milk. Spoon the sauce over the eggs and spinach. Sprinkle with the rest of the cheese and brown under the broiler. Serve hot.

Spinach with Cream
(*Épinards à la Crème*)

2 pounds spinach
Salt
¼ cup (½ stick) butter
Freshly ground black pepper

Freshly grated nutmeg
1 cup heavy cream *or* crème
  fraîche

Blanch the spinach in slightly salted, boiling water for 5 minutes. Drain well and chop. Heat the butter in a heavy pan and add the spinach. Season with pepper and nutmeg and turn the spinach in the hot butter. Stir in the cream. When the cream is well blended, serve the spinach with garlic-flavored warm bread.

Squash

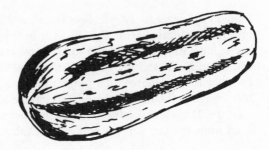

Squash Provence-Style
(Courge à la Provençale)

Serves 4

1 2–3 pound squash
3 tablespoons olive oil
1 tablespoon melted butter
1 onion, sliced
1 pound tomatoes, chopped
2–4 cloves garlic, finely chopped
1 teaspoon chopped basil

1 teaspoon chopped oregano
2 teaspoons chopped parsley
Salt
Freshly ground black pepper
1 cup vegetable stock
1 cup dry red wine

Peel the squash, remove the seeds and cut into small chunks or slices. Heat the oil and butter in a heavy pan and gently sauté the onion until transparent. Add the tomatoes and garlic and turn in the oil for 3 minutes. Add the squash pieces, herbs and salt and pepper to taste. Turn in the oil for 5 minutes. Add the stock and wine and cook together until the squash is tender. Continue to cook if you want the sauce to thicken.

Baked Squash
(Courge au Four)

Serves 4

1 2–3 pound squash
4 tablespoons olive oil
2–4 cloves garlic, sliced
Salt
Freshly ground black pepper
2 teaspoons chopped sage
1 tablespoon chopped parsley

½ cup vegetable stock
Butter
3 tablespoons whole wheat
  breadcrumbs
2 tablespoons grated parmesan
  or cheddar cheese

Preheat the oven to 400°F. Peel the squash, remove the seeds and cut into small chunks. Heat the oil in a heavy pan and gently sauté the garlic for 2 minutes. Add the squash and turn in the oil for 3 minutes. Season with salt and pepper to taste and add the herbs and stock. Cook together for 3 minutes then pour into a well-buttered ovenproof dish. Mix together the breadcrumbs and cheese and spread over the squash mixture. Drizzle 2–3 tablespoons of melted butter over and bake in the oven until the top is crisp and golden (about 30 minutes).

String Beans

String Bean Salad
(Salade d'Haricots Verts)   Serves 4

1 pound young string beans
Salt
Olive oil
Wine vinegar

Freshly ground black pepper
2 teaspoons chopped tarragon
1 teaspoon chopped chives

Trim the beans and boil in slightly salted water until just tender (a few minutes only). Drain. Make up a vinaigrette dressing to taste with olive oil, vinegar, salt and pepper. Pour over just enough to cover the beans and turn them in the dressing. Arrange on a serving dish and garnish with the chopped herbs. The beans can be eaten warm or allowed to chill for 30 minutes.

String Beans with Tomatoes
(Haricots Verts aux Tomates)   Serves 4

2 tablespoons melted butter
2 tablespoons olive oil
2-4 cloves garlic, sliced
1 pound string beans, trimmed
  and sliced
1½ cups chopped tomatoes

1 tablespoon chopped basil
1 tablespoon chopped parsley
Salt
Freshly ground black pepper
1 cup vegetable stock
1 cup dry red wine

Heat the butter and oil in a heavy pan and gently sauté the garlic for 2 minutes. Add the beans, tomatoes, herbs and salt and pepper to taste. Turn in the oil for 5 minutes. Add the stock and wine and cover. Cook over low heat for 10–15 minutes.

String Beans with Garlic
(Haricots Verts à l'Ail)

Serves 4

1 pound string beans
Salt
4 tablespoons melted butter
2–4 cloves garlic, finely chopped

2 tablespoons whole wheat
   breadcrumbs
Freshly ground black pepper
A few finely chopped sage leaves

Trim the beans. Make sure they are firm and snap when broken. Break the beans in half. Blanch in slightly salted, boiling water until just tender (about 10 minutes). Drain. Heat the butter in a heavy pan and gently sauté the garlic for 2 minutes. Add the breadcrumbs and season with salt and pepper to taste. Sauté together until the breadcrumbs begin to brown. Do not allow the butter to burn. Remove from the heat and put in the beans. Turn quickly in the garlic butter. Serve garnished with the chopped herb.

String Beans with Turnips
(Haricots Verts aux Navets)

Serves 4

½ pound turnips
½ pound string beans
Salt
2 tablespoons melted butter
2 tablespoons olive oil

1 onion, sliced
1¼ cups chopped tomatoes
Freshly ground black pepper
½ cup dry wine

Peel the turnips and cut into small pieces. Trim the beans and snap in half. Cook both vegetables in separate pans of slightly salted water until they are almost tender. Remove the vegetables and keep the liquid to one side. Heat the butter and oil in a heavy pan and gently sauté the onion until transparent. Add the tomatoes and turn in the oil for 5 minutes. Add the parcooked vegetables and season with salt and pepper to taste. Add the wine and any of the liquid needed from the parcooked vegetables to make a sauce. Cover and cook over low heat for 10 minutes.

String Beans with Mushrooms
(Haricots Verts au Forestier)   Serves 4

The title of the dish refers to the wild mushrooms that grow in woods and forests and which form a natural part of the country cuisine in such areas. Use any large mushrooms that may be available.

1 pound string beans	½ pound mushrooms, sliced
Salt	2–4 cloves garlic, sliced
3 tablespoons melted butter	Freshly ground black pepper
1 tablespoon olive oil	2 teaspoons chopped parsley

Trim the beans and snap in half. Blanch in slightly salted, boiling water until just tender. Drain. Heat the butter and oil in a heavy pan and gently sauté the mushrooms for 2 minutes. Add the garlic and season with salt and pepper to taste. Sauté together for 3 minutes. Add the beans and turn in the mushrooms for a further 3 minutes. Serve garnished with chopped parsley or any herb.

String Bean Gratin
(*Gratin de Haricots Verts*)

1 pound string beans
Salt
2 tablespoons melted butter
½ pound small mushrooms,
   sliced thickly
Freshly ground black pepper
2 teaspoons chopped parsley

3 tablespoons whole wheat
   breadcrumbs
2 tablespoons grated gruyère *or*
   cheddar cheese
1 teaspoon chopped rosemary
2 tablespoons olive oil

Trim the beans and snap in half. Blanch in slightly salted, boiling water for 5 minutes. Drain. Preheat the oven to 400°F. Heat the butter in a heavy pan and gently sauté the mushrooms for 2 minutes. Season with salt and pepper to taste and stir in the parsley. Add the beans and turn in the butter for 3 minutes. Put in a greased ovenproof dish. Mix together the breadcrumbs, cheese and rosemary and spread over the bean and mushroom mixture. Trickle the oil over and bake in the oven for 30 minutes or until the top is crisp and golden.

Sweet Corn

Grilled Sweet Corn with Tarragon Butter
(Epis de Maïs Grillé au Beurre d'Estragon) Serves 4

½ cup dry white wine
2 teaspoons fresh tarragon leaves
2 cups (4 sticks) butter, softened

Salt
Freshly ground black pepper
4 ears sweet corn

The tarragon butter may be made in advance or just before the sweet corn is grilled. Put the wine and herbs in a small saucepan and bring to a boil. Lower the heat and allow to reduce until about 3 tablespoons of liquid remain. Allow to cool for a few minutes. Add the softened butter and salt and pepper to taste. Mix together with a small whisk or fork to make a smooth thick cream. Keep to one side.

Pull off the husks of the sweet corn and cook the ears in plenty of boiling water for 5 minutes. Drain. Spread with a little of the tarragon butter and cook under the broiler until golden (15–20 minutes), turning the ears so that they are evenly broiled. Serve with the rest of the tarragon butter.

Naturally this method lends itself to barbecuing.

Sweet Corn Salad
(Salade de Maïs) Serves 4

1 cup canned *or* frozen sweet
  corn
Pat butter
Salt
Freshly ground black pepper
A few fresh tarragon leaves

1 small iceberg lettuce
1 small green pepper, seeded
  and diced
2 small tomatoes, cut in pieces
1 apple, cored and cut in small
  pieces

Cook the sweet corn in its juice or a small amount of water until it is well warmed through (5–7 minutes). Drain and stir in the butter, salt and pepper to taste, and tarragon. Keep warm.

Meanwhile, prepare the rest of the salad. Arrange the lettuce around the edge of the salad bowl. Stir the green pepper, tomato and apple into the warm sweet corn. Put this mixture in the middle of the lettuce leaves. Serve while still warm.

Swiss Chard

Swiss chard belongs to the same family as beets. It is widely cultivated in France, especially around the Lyons area. It is known by various names including *bette*, *blette* and *poirée à carde*.

Swiss Chard with Butter Sauce
(*Bettes au Beurre*)   Serves 4

The simplest way to prepare any green vegetable is to boil it until just tender (a few minutes only) and then to gently braise it in butter with a little seasoning.

1½ pounds Swiss chard leaves
Salt
2 tablespoons melted butter

1 tablespoon chopped parsley
Freshly ground black pepper

Wash the green leaves and strip the leaf from the stem. Blanch in a pan of boiling, slightly salted water until tender (about 10 minutes). Drain thoroughly and slice. Heat the butter in a heavy pan and stir in the Swiss chard. Add the parsley and season lightly with a little pepper. Stir together for 2 minutes.

Swiss Chard and Apple Pie
(*Tourte de Blea*)

This is a savory variation of the classic Provençal dish.

For the pastry:
1 cup whole wheat flour
1 cup self-rising flour
¼ cup (½ stick) margarine

¼ cup (½ stick) butter
Pinch salt

For the filling:
2¾ cups Swiss chard leaves
1¾ cups peeled and sliced
   cooking apples
2 tablespoons melted butter
½ onion, sliced
2 cloves garlic, finely chopped
1 cup cooked navy beans
1 teaspoon chopped thyme

1 teaspoon chopped sage
1 teaspoon chopped basil
1 tablespoon pine nuts *or* sliced
   almonds
Salt
Freshly ground black pepper
Milk for glazing

Make sure all the items for making the pastry are chilled. Mix the flours together in a bowl. Cut the margarine and butter into pieces. Sift the flour with the salt and add the pieces of margarine and butter. Make into crumbs with the fingertips. Sprinkle 2 tablespoons of cold water over and cut into the flour mixture with a knife. Add a little more water to make a smooth dough which comes away cleanly from the sides of the bowl. Wrap in plastic wrap and allow to rest in the refrigerator for 30 minutes.

Wash and trim the Swiss chard leaves and blanch in boiling water for 6 minutes. Drain thoroughly and chop. Cook apple slices in a little water for 5 minutes. Drain. Heat the butter in a heavy pan and sauté the onion until golden. Add the garlic and turn in the butter for 2 minutes. Add the Swiss chard, apples, beans, herbs, nuts and salt and pepper to taste. Cook together for 5 minutes. Preheat the oven to 400°F.

Roll out the pastry with the help of a little flour. Use two-thirds of it to line the bottom and sides of a greased 9½-inch pie dish. Put in the filling ingredients. Cover with the top crust. This should be joined to the base by moistening with a little water and pressing the two edges together with a fork. Prick holes in the lid and brush with milk to glaze. Bake in the oven until golden (about 30 minutes).

Swiss Chard with Eggs
(*Bettes en Gâteau*)   Serves 4

1½ pounds Swiss chard leaves
2 tablespoons olive oil
1 tablespoon melted butter
1 bunch scallions, sliced
1½ cups sliced mushrooms
Salt
Freshly ground black pepper

1 teaspoon chopped parsley
1 teaspoon chopped thyme
2 tablespoons whole wheat flour
3 eggs, beaten
1 egg yolk
⅔ cup milk

Preheat the oven to 400°F. Wash the Swiss chard and strip the green leaf from the stems. Blanch the leaves in boiling water for 5 minutes. Drain thoroughly and chop. Heat the oil and butter in a heavy pan and sauté the scallions for 3 minutes. Add the mushrooms, salt and pepper to taste and turn in the oil for 3 minutes. Add the Swiss chard and herbs and mix well over low heat for a few minutes. Remove from the heat. In a separate bowl, beat the flour into the eggs and egg yolk. Stir in the milk. Pour into the Swiss chard mixture. Put the mixture in a greased ovenproof dish and bake in the oven until the eggs are set and the top begins to turn golden (30–40 minutes). Allow to cool for a few minutes before serving.

Swiss Chard Gratin
(*Gratin de Bettes*)

Serves 4

1 pound Swiss chard leaves
Salt
Freshly ground black pepper
3 cups sliced mushrooms
1 cup heavy cream *or* crème
    fraîche

Freshly grated nutmeg
4 tablespoons grated gruyère *or*
    cheddar cheese

Preheat the oven to 375°F. Wash and trim the Swiss chard leaves and blanch in boiling water for 5 minutes. Drain thoroughly and chop. Put half the Swiss chard in the bottom of a greased ovenproof dish and season with a little salt and pepper. Put in the sliced mushrooms and cover with the rest of the Swiss chard. Season again. Pour the cream over and sprinkle with a little nutmeg. Cover with grated cheese and bake in the oven until the top is golden (30–40 minutes).

Tomatoes

Tomatoes are widely cultivated in France, especially in the valley of the Garonne. The south produces the large tomato known as the Mediterranean tomato, which is ideal for stuffing.

Tomato and Vegetable Soup
(*Potage à la Liégeoise*)   Serves 4

This is a nourishing soup typical of the industrial north.

2 tablespoons olive oil
2 tablespoons melted butter
1 onion, sliced
2 stalks celery, sliced
2 tablespoons chopped parsley
1¼ cups chopped tomatoes
1⅓ cups chopped potatoes

Handful chopped fresh herbs
Salt
Freshly ground black pepper
1 teaspoon chopped sage
2 cloves garlic, crushed
6 cups vegetable stock *or* water
1 tablespoon tomato purée

Heat the oil and butter in a heavy pan and sauté the onion until just golden. Add the celery, parsley, tomatoes, potatoes, herbs and salt and pepper to taste. Sauté together for 5 minutes. Add the sage and garlic and turn in the oil. Add the stock and tomato purée and stir together. Cover and simmer for 30 minutes. Serve with sautéed or warm crusty bread.

Tomato and Zucchini Summer Soup
(*Potage Glacé à la Catalane*)

Serves 4

The ancient province of Catalonia straddles the Pyrenees, having both French and Spanish regions. This cold soup, which has relatives across the border, is delicious during a hot spell.

1 pound tomatoes, chopped
2 zucchini, sliced
3-inch piece cucumber, sliced
1 small onion, chopped
2 cloves garlic, sliced
1 stalk celery, chopped
4 tablespoons olive oil

Pinch saffron
1 cup milk *or* natural yogurt
3¾ cups vegetable stock
Salt
Freshly ground black pepper
Pinch cayenne pepper

Purée all the vegetables in a blender or food processor. Pour into a bowl. Stir in the oil. Dissolve the saffron in the milk. It should turn a nice yellow-orange color. Stir into the puréed vegetables. Add the stock and seasoning to taste. Stir well together and chill. Serve cold.

Tomato Soup
(*Potage aux Tomates*)

Serves 4–6

2 tablespoons olive oil
2 tablespoons melted butter
1 small onion, finely chopped
2 pounds tomatoes, chopped
½ pound potatoes, chopped
1 teaspoon salt

½ teaspoon freshly ground black pepper
1 teaspoon soft brown sugar
7 cups thin stock *or* water
1 tablespoon chopped parsley

Heat the oil and butter in a heavy soup pot and sauté the onion until transparent. Add the tomatoes and potatoes and mix well with the oil. Sprinkle with salt, pepper and sugar. Add the stock and bring to a boil. Cover and turn down the heat to simmer until the vegetables are soft. Purée in a blender or food processor. Serve garnished with chopped parsley.

Stuffed Tomatoes
(*Tomates Farcies*)

Serves 4

8 large tomatoes
4 tablespoons olive oil
1 onion, finely chopped
2–4 cloves garlic, finely chopped
2 cups cooked rice
1 cup chopped walnuts *or* almonds

1 cup whole wheat breadcrumbs
1 teaspoon salt
½ teaspoon freshly ground black pepper
2 teaspoons chopped basil
1 tablespoon chopped parsley

Preheat the oven to 375°F. Wash the tomatoes and slice off the tops. Keep to one side. Scoop out the pulp and retain. Arrange the tomato shells on a greased baking dish. Heat the oil in a heavy pan and gently sauté the onion for 3 minutes. Add the garlic, rice, nuts, breadcrumbs and tomato pulp. Sprinkle with salt, pepper and herbs. Mix together and sauté for 5 minutes. Put some of the filling mixture in each of the tomato shells. Put the tops back on. Bake in the oven for 30 minutes.

Sautéed Tomatoes
(*Tomates Provençales*)

Serves 4

8 tomatoes
4 tablespoons olive oil
Salt
Freshly ground black pepper
2 cloves garlic, finely chopped
3 tablespoons whole wheat breadcrumbs

1 teaspoon chopped sage
1 teaspoon chopped oregano
1 teaspoon chopped thyme
1 teaspoon chopped parsley

Cut the tomatoes in halves. Heat the oil in a heavy pan and gently sauté the tomato halves. Sprinkle with a little salt and pepper. Cover the pan with a lid to prevent the oil from spattering. Remove the tomatoes and keep warm. Put the garlic in the hot oil and sauté for 2 minutes. Add the breadcrumbs and herbs. Sauté together for 3 minutes. Sprinkle over the sautéed tomatoes. Serve hot.

Tomatoes with Mushrooms
(*Tomates au Four*)

Serves 4

4 tablespoons olive oil
1 pound tomatoes, chopped
3 cups sliced mushrooms
2 cloves garlic, finely chopped
2 teaspoons chopped parsley
2 teaspoons chopped thyme
2 teaspoons chopped basil

Salt
Freshly ground black pepper
1 egg, beaten
4 tablespoons whole wheat
  breadcrumbs
2 tablespoons melted butter

Preheat the oven to 400°F. Heat the oil in a heavy pan and sauté the tomatoes for 3 minutes. Add the mushrooms, garlic, herbs and salt and pepper to taste. Sauté together for 3 minutes and then add the beaten egg. Stir well and pour into a greased ovenproof dish. Cover with the breadcrumbs. Trickle the melted butter over and bake in the oven until the top is crisp and golden (15–20 minutes).

Tomato Salad
(*Salade de Tomates*)

Serves 4

1 pound tomatoes, sliced
⅔ cup sliced scallions
1 tablespoon wine vinegar
1 teaspoon soft brown sugar
Salt
Freshly ground black pepper

½ teaspoon Dijon mustard
3 tablespoons olive oil
½–1 clove garlic, finely chopped
1 tablespoon chopped fresh basil
  or parsley

Arrange the tomatoes and scallions on a serving dish. Whisk together the vinegar, sugar, a good pinch of salt and pepper and the mustard. Gradually whisk in the oil, garlic and herbs until the sauce is well blended. Spoon over the tomatoes and onions. Cover and let stand for 1 hour.

Turnips

The turnip is generally used in France as a soup or stew vegetable like the carrot or onion. French cooks prefer the small white and purple turnip which has a mild, slightly sweet taste. The best turnips for this purpose are said to come from the area around Meaux.

Turnip Stew
(*Ragoût de Navets*)
Serves 4

1½ pounds turnips
Salt
3 tablespoons olive oil
1 onion, finely chopped
1 tablespoon whole wheat flour
1¼ cups chopped tomatoes

2 cloves garlic, finely chopped
Freshly ground black pepper
1 cup vegetable stock
1 teaspoon chopped sage
1 tablespoon chopped parsley

Peel the turnips and cut into small chunks. Blanch in boiling, slightly salted water for 5 minutes. Drain. Heat the oil in a heavy pan and gently sauté the onion until transparent. Stir in the flour and sauté together for 2 minutes. Add the tomatoes, garlic and turnips and season with salt and pepper to taste. Stir together for 5 minutes. Add the stock and sage to cover. Cook over low heat until the turnips are tender, adding more stock if necessary to prevent sticking. Serve garnished with the chopped parsley.

Turnips with Cream Sauce
(*Navets à la Crème*)   Serves 4

1½ pounds turnips
Salt
1 tablespoon butter
1 tablespoon whole wheat flour

½ cup milk
1½ cups cream
Freshly ground black pepper
1 tablespoon dry wine

Peel the turnips and cut into small chunks. Boil in a little slightly salted water until just tender. Drain and keep warm. Meanwhile, make the cream sauce. Melt the butter in a heavy saucepan over low heat. Stir in the flour and stir together for 2 minutes. Remove the roux from the heat. As soon as it has stopped bubbling, whisk in hot milk. Whisk well until it is well blended. Whisk in the cream. Season with salt and pepper and stir in the wine. Pour the cream sauce over the cooked turnips.

Turnip Gratin
(*Gratin de Navets*)   Serves 4

1½ pounds turnips
Salt
2 tablespoons melted butter
1 clove garlic, finely chopped
Freshly ground black pepper
1 teaspoon chopped sage
1 teaspoon chopped parsley

1 teaspoon chopped chervil
4 tablespoons grated gruyère *or* cheddar cheese
1 cup crème fraîche *or* natural yogurt
3 tablespoons whole wheat breadcrumbs

Preheat the oven to 400°F. Peel the turnips and cut into small chunks. Blanch in boiling, slightly salted water for 5 minutes. Drain. Heat the butter in a heavy pan and sauté the garlic for 2 minutes. Add the turnip pieces and sauté together for 2 minutes. Turn into a greased ovenproof dish. Season with salt and pepper and sprinkle the herbs over. Cover with the cheese and pour over the crème fraîche, spreading to cover as necessary. Cover with the breadcrumbs and bake in the oven until the top is crisp and golden (about 30 minutes).

Turnips with Herbs
(*Navets aux Fines Herbes*)

Serves 4

1½ pounds turnips
Salt
3 tablespoons melted butter
Freshly ground black pepper
1 teaspoon chopped sage
1 teaspoon chopped chives

1 teaspoon chopped tarragon
1 teaspoon chopped thyme *or*
   parsley
4-inch piece cucumber, sliced
2 tomatoes, sliced

Peel the turnips and cut into chunks. Boil in sightly salted water until just tender. Slice the turnip chunks. Heat the butter in a heavy pan over low heat. Add the turnip slices and season well with pepper. Turn in the butter for 3 minutes. Add the herbs and turn for 1 minute. Put onto a serving dish and garnish with cucumber and tomato slices.

Glazed Turnips
(*Navets Glacés*)

Serves 4

2 pounds small turnips
Salt
3 tablespoons butter

1 cup stock
1 tablespoon confectioner's sugar
Freshly ground black pepper

Peel the turnips and cut into small pieces. Cook in a pan of boiling, slightly salted water for 15 minutes. Drain. Put the butter in a heavy pan and melt over low heat. Add the turnips, stock and sugar and pepper to taste. Allow to simmer until all the liquid has evaporated and the turnips are coated in a thick syrup.

Zucchini

These small squash originally came from Italy and are also known in France as *courgerons* or *coucourzelles*. They have become an important ingredient in French cuisine, especially the southern style.

Zucchini Quiche
(*Quiche aux Courgettes*)

Serves 4

For the pastry:

1 cup whole wheat self-rising flour *or* 1 cup whole wheat flour and 1 teaspoon baking powder

Pinch salt

2½ tablespoons butter, cut in pieces

2½ tablespoons margarine, cut in pieces

1 teaspoon soft brown sugar

3 tablespoons cold water

1 tablespoon olive oil

For the filling:

3 tablespoons olive oil

1 small onion, sliced

1 clove garlic, finely chopped

1 pound zucchini, trimmed and sliced

Salt

Freshly ground black pepper

1 teaspoon chopped oregano

1 teaspoon chopped basil

2 eggs

3 tablespoons heavy cream *or* natural yogurt

First make the quiche pastry. Sift the flour with the salt in a mixing bowl. Cut the chilled butter and margarine into the flour with a knife. Make into crumbs with the fingertips. In a separate bowl dissolve the sugar in the water and stir in the oil. Gradually add this mixture to the flour until a soft, pliable dough is formed which comes away from the sides of the bowl. You may not need all of the liquid. Use flour to make into a ball. Wrap in plastic wrap and put in the refrigerator for 20 minutes. After 10 minutes preheat the oven to 400°F.

Meanwhile, make the filling. Heat the oil in a heavy pan and gently sauté the onion until transparent. Add the garlic and zucchini and turn in the oil for 3 minutes. Add salt and pepper to taste and the herbs. Sauté together for 5 minutes. Remove from the heat. Beat the eggs and cream together in a bowl.

Roll out the pastry on a floured board and place in a greased 8-9-inch quiche pan with a removable base. Pull the pastry up the sides of the pan. Prick all over with a fork. Bake in the oven until the pastry has set (5-7 minutes). Allow to cool for a few minutes.

Arrange the zucchini in the quiche base. Spoon in the egg and cream mixture to fill in any gaps and to just cover the zucchini. Bake in the oven for 30 minutes. Allow to cool for a few minutes before removing from the pan. Serve hot or cold.

Fried Zucchini
(*Courgettes à la Meunière*)   Serves 4

The French title of this dish (in the style of the miller's wife) refers to the method of coating the vegetable slices in flour before frying.

1 pound zucchini	1 tablespoon chopped parsley
Whole wheat flour	Lemon wedges
Oil for frying	

Trim the zucchini and cut in thick slices. Roll in the flour to coat on both sides. Fry in hot oil until golden on both sides. Drain on paper towels and put on a serving dish. Sprinkle the chopped parsley over and serve with lemon wedges.

Baked Zucchini
(*Courgettes au Four*)

Serves 4

4 tablespoons olive oil
1 onion, sliced
1¼ cups chopped tomatoes
2 cups sliced celery
Salt
Freshly ground black pepper
2-4 cloves garlic, finely chopped

A few sage leaves
1 teaspoon chopped basil
1 pound zucchini
3-4 tablespoons whole wheat breadcrumbs
2 tablespoons natural yogurt *or* crème fraîche

Preheat the oven to 400°F. In a heavy pan heat the olive oil and gently sauté the onion until almost golden. Add the tomatoes and celery and turn in the oil. Season with salt and pepper to taste and add the garlic and herbs. Turn in the oil over low heat until the tomatoes are tender.

Trim the zucchini and slice thinly. Arrange in a greased, shallow ovenproof dish. Pour the tomato and celery mixture over and cover with the breadcrumbs. Spread with the yogurt and bake in the oven until the top is crisp and golden (25–35 minutes).

Pickled Zucchini
(*Courgettes à la Grecque*)

Serves 6

This dish uses the Greek style of marinating vegetables for use in a salad or hors d'oeuvres.

1 pound zucchini
Salt
1¼ cups water
½ cup olive oil
Juice of 1 lemon
1 teaspoon chopped oregano
1 teaspoon chopped parsley

Freshly ground black pepper
1 small onion, sliced
½ small green pepper, sliced
1 clove garlic, finely chopped
1 tomato, chopped in small pieces
12 black olives

Cut the zucchini in thick slices and boil in slightly salted water until just tender (a few minutes). Drain. In a heavy pan mix together the water, olive oil, lemon juice, herbs and salt and pepper to taste. Heat together gently for 5 minutes and allow the liquid to cool. Put the zucchini slices in a bowl with the onion, green pepper and garlic and pour the marinade over. Let stand in a cool place for a day or overnight. Next day drain off any excess marinade and serve with tomato and olives.

Zucchini Gratin
(*Gratin de Courgettes*)   Serves 4

3 tablespoons olive oil
1 small onion, sliced
1 pound zucchini, trimmed and
   thinly sliced
Salt
Freshly ground black pepper
1 tablespoon chopped parsley
2 cloves garlic, finely chopped
3 tablespoons whole wheat
   breadcrumbs

3 tablespoons grated gruyère *or*
   cheddar cheese
1 teaspoon chopped marjoram
1 egg, beaten
3 tablespoons crème fraîche *or*
   natural yogurt
½ teaspoon paprika

Preheat the oven to 400°F. Heat the oil in a heavy pan and gently sauté the onion until transparent. Add the zucchini and salt and pepper to taste. Turn in the oil for 3 minutes. Add the parsley and garlic and cook together for 2 more minutes. In a separate bowl mix together the breadcrumbs, cheese, marjoram and beaten egg. Put the zucchini mixture in an ovenproof dish. Spread the breadcrumb mixture over and bake in the oven for 10 minutes. Remove and spread the crème fraîche over and sprinkle on the paprika. Continue baking in the oven for a further 20 minutes.

Stewed Zucchini
(*Ragoût de Courgettes*)

Serves 4

4 tablespoons olive oil
1 onion, finely chopped
1¼ cups chopped tomatoes
1 pound zucchini, trimmed and
  sliced
½ pound mushrooms, sliced
2–4 cloves garlic, finely chopped

1 stalk celery, sliced
Handful of black olives, pitted
Salt
Freshly ground black pepper
2 teaspoons chopped basil
2 teaspoons chopped parsley

Heat the oil in a heavy pan and gently sauté the onion until transparent. Add the tomatoes and zucchini and turn in the oil for 2 minutes. Add the mushrooms, garlic and celery and olives and cook together for a few minutes over low heat. Add the salt and pepper to taste and the herbs. Cover and allow the dish to stew, adding a little water or vegetable stock if needed.

Zucchini with Onions
(*Courgettes aux Ciboules*)

Serves 4

2 tablespoons olive oil
2 tablespoons melted butter
1 pound zucchini, trimmed and
  sliced
Salt

Freshly ground black pepper
1 bunch scallions, sliced
1 teaspoon chopped oregano
1 tablespoon chopped parsley

Heat the oil and butter in a heavy pan and lightly sauté the zucchini for 2 minutes. Sprinkle on the seasoning to taste and add the onions. Turn in the oil for 3 minutes and add the herbs. Cover and cook together over low heat for a few minutes until the zucchini are just tender.

Zucchini with Cream Sauce
(*Courgettes à la Crème*)

Serves 4

3 tablespoons melted butter
1 tablespoon olive oil
1 pound zucchini, trimmed and
  sliced
Salt
Freshly ground black pepper

1-2 cloves garlic, finely chopped
1 cup heavy cream *or* natural
  yogurt
½ cup vegetable stock
2 teaspoons chopped mint

Heat the butter and oil in a heavy pan and lightly sauté the zucchini for 3 minutes. Sprinkle with salt and pepper to taste and add the garlic. Turn in the oil for 2 minutes. Add the cream and stock. Cover and cook over low heat for a few minutes until the zucchini are just tender. Serve garnished with the chopped mint.

Glossary

ail	garlic
artichaut	artichoke
asperge	asparagus
basilic	basil
beignet	fritter
bette	Swiss chard
betterave	beet
beurre	butter
blea	Swiss chard (Provence)
bourbonnais	Bourbon
braisé	braised
en branche	whole stalks
brouillé	scrambled (of eggs)
carotte	carrot
à la catalane	in the style of Catalonia
céleri	celery
céleri-rave	celeriac
cerfeuil	chervil
champignon	mushroom
chèvre	goat
chou	cabbage
chou-fleur	cauliflower
chou rouge	red cabbage
choux de Bruxelles	Brussels sprouts
ciboule	scallion
concombre	cucumber
courge	squash
à la crème	with cream or cream sauce
crêpe	pancake
cresson	watercress
croquette	croquette, patty
épinards	spinach

endive	chicory
farci	stuffed
fenouil	fennel
fermière	farmer's wife
feuille	leaf
fève	fava bean
fines herbes	culinary herbs
au four	baked (in the oven)
fromage	cheese
galette	pancake, crêpe, cake
gâteau	cake
glacé	glazed, chilled, frozen
gratin	baked dish, topped with cheese or breadcrumbs
haricot	navy bean
haricot verts	string beans
jeudi	Thursday
laitue	lettuce
légume	vegetable
à la liégeoise	in the style of Liège, Belgium
maïs	sweet corn
marron	chestnut
menthe	mint
Midi	south of France
navet	turnip
noix	walnut
oeuf	egg
oignon	onion
oseille	sorrel
pain	bread
panais	parsnip
pâté	pie, cake, patty
paysanne	country woman
petits pois	small peas
pissenlit	dandelion (literally "piss in bed")
pistou	paste made from basil, garlic and parmesan cheese
poché	poached
pois	pea
pois chiche	chick pea
poireau	leek
poivron	green or red sweet pepper
polonais	Polish

pomme	apple
pomme de terre	potato
potage	soup
potiron	pumpkin
quiche	quiche
ragoût	stew
riz	rice
salade	salad, lettuce
tomate	tomato
tourte	pie (Provence)
velouté	velvety, creamy (as of a white sauce)
vendanges	grape harvest
vert	green
vinaigrette	sauce or dressing made with wine vinegar and olive oil and seasoned